MAGGIE ST....DER

"The Girl with the Glasses"

I hope you enjoy my story!

An Autobiography

With all good wishes!
Maggie x

First published in 2001 by
Showbiz Publications
P O Box 692A
Surbiton
Surrey
KT5 8DZ

E-mail: MJ48ALPHA@AOL.com

ISBN 0 9540587 1 2

Designed and produced by
The Short Run Book Company Limited
St Stephen's House
Arthur Road
Windsor
Berkshire SL4 1RY

FOREWORD

by Sir Cliff Richard, OBE

It was the Vernons Girls who, way back in the late 1950's gave me the very confidence boost I needed. 'You've got the sexiest bum in the business' they said. 'Go out there and shake it!'

Well, I've been shaking it ever since – although not so much recently!

Maggie – the one with the specs – and all the Vernons gang were so supportive of pimply little upstarts like Marty Wilde and me. When we were terrified at the thought of performing on those early *'Oh Boy'* t/v shows, Maggie and the girls were terrific and made us feel good, despite the fact that we were probably terrible – well I certainly was!!

Rehearsals for those shows were at Canonbury Lane, near Islington and it was like having a party every week. Everything was such fun – do you remember those breakfasts round the corner, Maggie?

Somehow, around 30 years have slipped by before we worked together again – at *The Event* at Wembley Stadium in 1989. Not only were we all able to stand, but the girls, wearing hot pants and performing to 140,000 people, looked fabulous.

Apart from the 'bum wiggle', there's something else I have to thank Maggie for. I'd always been a bit self conscious about wearing specs – but there was Maggie setting a new fashion trend. Specs were OK! On Maggie they looked cool and that was good enough for me.

So thank you Maggie and thank you girls. We started our careers together and it was such unpretentious fun. Who'd have thought we'd still be going strong nearly 45 years later!

Good Luck!

My Love

Cliff

1st June 2001.

JIM KENNEDY

An Acknowledgement

To my darling husband Jim for his skill in transcribing my scribbles, my jottings and my ramblings into the book form you are about to read. In addition, he battered my befuddled brain into remembering places, names and events – many from over 40 years ago – not an easy task!

For that – my love, appreciation and gratitude

* * * * * * *

Further thanks and much love go to the following for their help in producing photographs and material which have greatly helped in producing this book.

British Pathé

Colin Hunt

Marty Wilde

Joe Brown

Sir Cliff Richard

Max & Anthony Bygraves

Colin Wilkinson

Ann Simmonds

Jan Alderson

Maggie

CONTENTS

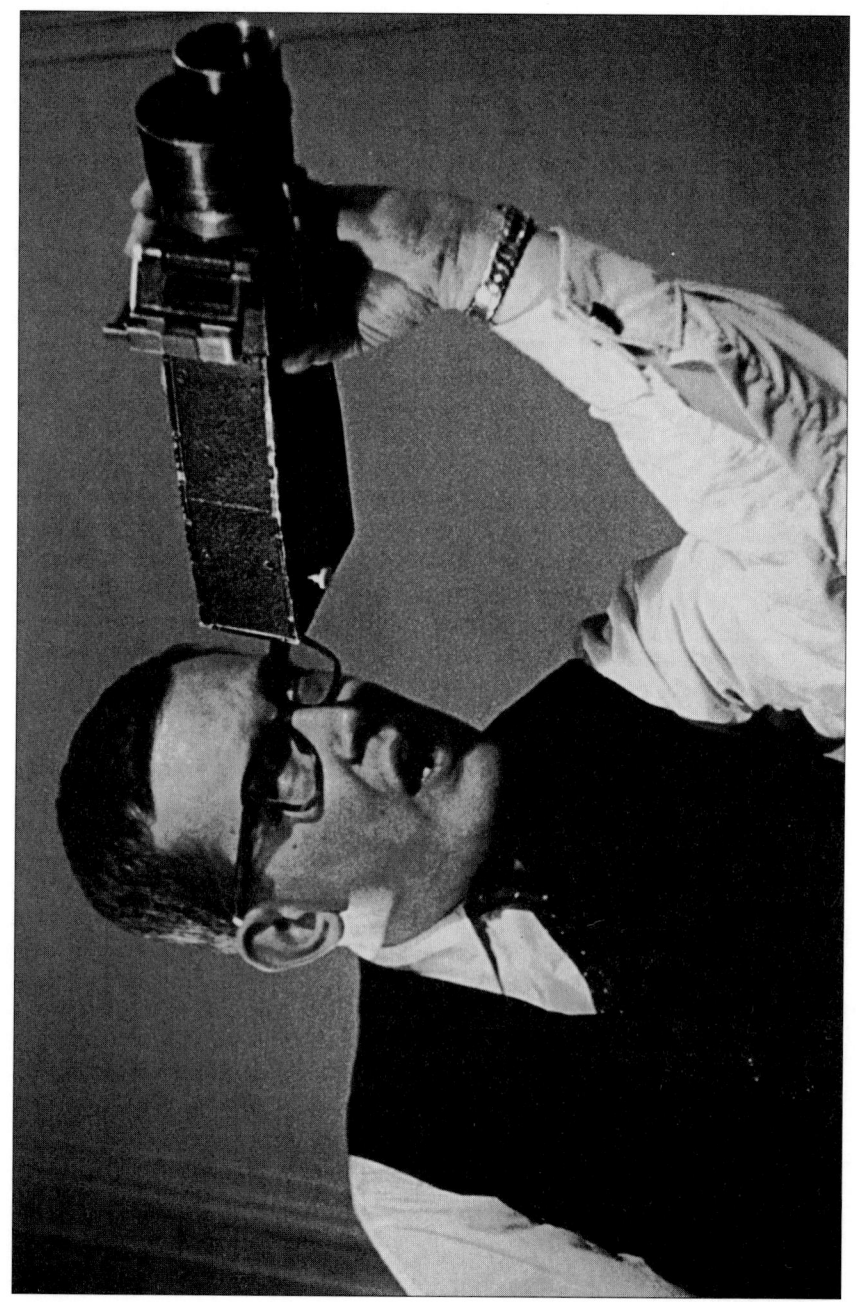

The man who began it all for me – producer/director Jack Good

PROLOGUE

The door opened and Jack Good entered the room. To those who should have known better, he was nothing more than a pleasant looking man with a round, almost avuncular figure and a face borrowed from the classroom of 'Tom Brown's Schooldays' – bland, scholastic and sporting a permanent, almost cheeky, grin! To link such an unpretentious being to the powerful iconic producer of the most innovative pop programme of the generation – T.V.'s 'Six-Five Special' – would have been unthinkable but we, the sixteen strong members (plus two reserves) of the all singing, all dancing vocal group, The Vernons Girls, knew better and when he began to speak, we hung on his every syllable.

We had already appeared, more than once, on the programme and therefore knew, first hand, the genius that the man undoubtedly was. Neither were we fooled by the untidy, dishevelled appearance he portrayed for we were aware, as was almost every emerging rock'n'roll wannabee desperate to be recognised by this new, exciting medium, that within the palm of his hand was the power to make and break instant stars overnight. Jack Good was not just an icon – he was God!!!

It was a warm July day in the summer of 1958 and our chaperone, Miss Finegan, had casually mentioned that Good wished to speak to us regarding the possibility of our appearing in a brand new pop show he was about to produce – and so we gathered in a room within the Bluecoat Chambers in Liverpool, to hear what the great man had to say. It was no exaggeration to reveal that our fingers were crossed just a little tighter and our hearts beat just a little faster in hopeful anticipation of what may be coming our way. We were not to be disappointed and for me, this proved to be one of the most significant moments of my life – although not in the way I initially expected.

It was to make me instantly recognisable, a personality in my own right and a celebrity in show business – something I had never dreamed of. How did this miracle happen? How did the skinny, bespectacled 'Scouser' from Birkenhead suddenly make the big time? And why, when the suggestion to create this metamorphosis was made, did I flood with tears, anticipating the absolute worst which would, almost certainly, include expulsion from the singing group that had become the fulcrum of my life ? Read on, dear Reader – read on!!!

Jack Good spoke with a passion, somewhat greater than we had heard from him before. He described the concept of his new show, outlining its style and presentation. It was to be fast and seamless, exciting and breathtaking. It was a blueprint for a pop show that had never been seen before and would effectively outdate every other modern music production at present in transmission including, he added, his much beloved 'Six-Five Special'. Finally, he paused for a moment – perhaps to take breath or more likely, knowing his penchant for the theatrical – for dramatic effect, before uttering the lines we now desperately longed to hear....."and alongside some others I have in mind, I would like The Vernons Girls to be resident for the entire series!!" Again, a pause to allow the impact of what he had just said, time to implode into our minds and comprehension before asking, unnecessarily, the question none of us even bothered to answer "Do you mind being famous?"

His smile broadened imperceptibly and his eyes twinkled at the sight of sixteen Vernons Girls (plus two reserves) wanting to explode in the joy of the moment, yet struggling to retain the discipline and the dignity so meticulously instilled in us since our inception. Nevertheless, he correctly interpreted the look on our faces as unconditional acceptance and, gentleman to the very last, he approached each of us individually to shake hands and wish us luck. He approached me and took my outstretched hand in his. "Well done" he said and half turned away. As if in afterthought, he suddenly looked back at me and said "And you, young lady, will keep on your glasses!!!". His words hit me like a sledgehammer. All the joy I had experienced at his announcement, all the excitement that had surged through me at his invitation to join the show, dissolved as if by the flick of a switch and my legs turned to jelly. I was devastated and I fought back the tears which threatened to engulf me. His words burned into my brain again and again and, in the weeks leading up the opening show, I lived a life of torture. I knew what was going to happen, I told myself. Who had ever heard of a singer and dancer on TV who actually wore *glasses*! People would snigger and, worse still, laugh out loud and Mr. Good would eventually remove me from my present position on the front line and find a place for me well hidden in the back row before finally asking me to leave the group – because I had become an embarrassment – a laughing stock!!

I was so unhappy imagining the disgrace about to befall me and tears became a daily part of my life leading up to the very first showing of the opening production of 'Oh Boy', as it was to be called. From the moment the band struck up the introductory fanfare heralding the dawn of a great new pop extravaganza, the show was a smash! During the times it occupied the country's TV screens, the streets emptied and pubs, cafes and restaurants became deserted. Whole families became glued to their sets, transfixed by what they saw before them and revelling in the firmament of new stars that were being unveiled before their eyes. Marty Wilde, Cliff Richard, Billy Fury, Vince Eager, Gene Vincent, Shirley Bassey, Conway Twitty, The Dallas Boys, Eddie Cochrane, Johnny Cash, Brenda Lee, Jerry Keller plus many, many more and the fan mail began to roll in the thousands.

To my utter amazement, great relief and absolute joy, a high percentage of fan letters received were simply addressed to 'The Girl with the Glasses' and I began to realise that Jack Good, with his unerring eye for a great gimmick, had realised the potential in using my glasses to propel me 'out of the chorus' and into public acclaim. I was recognised in the streets throughout the UK. I signed autographs, appeared on chat shows and was elevated to a status I had never thought possible. Jack Good had made me a personality in my own right and the character he created in the late fifties still lives on to this day. To him, I owe a debt of gratitude – but in doing so realise that, perhaps, I am 'jumping the gun' in terms of recounting the story of my life, so let me return to the very beginning when it all began and, with the help of some wonderful photographs from my album which only serve to convince me, time and time again that the whole adventure really happened, relate the happenings of what has been a wonderfully exciting life in which I have met and worked with many, if not most of the great stars worldwide from the past and indeed, the present. I hope, so much, that you enjoy my stories of the great days of pop music from the early fifties, the magical decade of the sixties and through the years to the present day. All has been made possible by some talent, a lot of luck and a very special man who really began it all by demanding "Young lady – you will keep on your glasses!!"

Thanks Jack – I owe you!

CHAPTER 1

Growing up in Birkenhead

Age is a simple three letter word that conjures up a multitude of interpretations. To some it represents a phobia and the thought of conceding to the march of time strikes terror into their very souls. To others, it is an obsession where the years of one's existence are spoken with great reverence and pride – as if achieving a personal attainment akin to a degree from some University. To me however, it is simply a contest – a joke!

Today, I consider myself so very fortunate to be still working – The Vernons Girls are still in demand (now as a threesome) and although our ages remain constant, it is noted that our audiences appear to be somewhat older! Increasingly, too, the phone rings to book me as a speaker, recalling my life in show business as both a Vernons Girl and a Ladybird and to relate profiles of some of the star names whose careers were intrinsically linked to mine – Benny Hill, Max Bygraves, Rolf Harris, Norman Wisdom and more.

To my (and our) great amusement, however, the introduction, whether it be as solo performer or collectively with the girls, is always followed by a scrutiny from the audience that borders on the hilarious. The vision of glamour we try so hard to sustain is dissected piece by piece from head to toe. The hair.... has it been dyed or, worse still, could it be a wig? The teeth..... surely can't be her own, must be false! Face..... where are the wrinkles? Could be good make up – but no, must be a tuck! Boobs..... ah, good job there. Great scaffolding and what about the legs? How did she manage to keep her legs looking like that? Not fair – no varicose veins, no cellulite. God – how old must she be? And so we go into phase two, when calculators appear. Now let's see. She began singing in the late fifties – so that must make her——? I am normally well into my talk, or singing, before the audience decide to give up the mathematical gymnastics and settle down to enjoy what is on offer and, thankfully, at the end of the showpiece, they decide that age doesn't come into it – the lady can still perform and still look good into the bargain.

To confuse the issue, however, I throw all their calculations into disarray by finally letting them into my ultimate secret – I am actually – still – only 45 years old! What I don't reveal, however, is that I have remained at that age for quite some time, and will do, I hope, for many more years to come. If it was good enough for Jack Benny who died late in life at the age of 39 – then it is good enough for me!

I was born in Grangemount Maternity Hospital, Birkenhead on 9th January, nineteen hundred and 'time-to-get-your-calculators-out again! My mum and dad were better known to all as Cissie and John Stredder and, having already produced a son – also named John and six years my senior – it was a great joy for them to welcome a daughter (me!) into the world. I was christened Margaret Elizabeth, and our first family home was in Hope Street, Birkenhead. Whoever named it Hope Street must have had a depraved sense of humour for it was little more than a street of despair, a breathing, living slum. Damp, dilapidated buildings that should have been condemned many years before, still stood in rotting decay and, when World War II broke out years later, the German bombers did the job the local Council wouldn't – and flattened it!

Thankfully we were not to suffer the miseries of Hope Street for long, and within weeks, had moved in with my Nan, who lived in a delightful 3 bedroomed semi-detached house in the northern end of the town. It was to prove an idyllic time for me, for not only did I have the joy of a garden (both back and front) and an inside loo – something new to me, for the Hope Street toilet was situated at the bottom of the yard – but was given my own bedroom where I could close the door and dream in total privacy.

Sadly, the happiness was not to last long for war clouds were gathering and before very long, nightly raids of German bombers blitzed the docks which seemed to surround us. At the sound of the air raid sirens, we would leave our lovely home to seek sanctuary in the communal, newly erected air raid shelters. One night, the sounds of explosions from the falling bombs seemed just a little closer than usual and when we emerged at the "all clear", we were to find that the house, which had given us so much love and happiness, had been reduced to a blackened shell.

My recollection of that moment is vague but I can, amazingly, vividly recall the following day being held securely in the arms of my Dad and wrapped for warmth in a Chenille table cloth (in those days everyone had one) viewing what was left of our home. The front section had gone completely and where my lovely bedroom had been 24 hours earlier, was nothing more than a gaping hole from which perched, precariously, the remains of my black iron bedstead.

We moved in with my Auntie May who lived in Craven Place, situated just behind the Gaumont Cinema but it was not a happy homecoming for she could be (and generally was) an unkind lady, to the point of being very cruel. She had two sons, not much older than me, and because all my belongings had perished in the bombing, I found I had to wear, and share, their clothes for some time after and was regularly seen wearing ill fitting school shirts, trousers and braces. If I appeared to be a 'girl turned boy', two streets away lived a boy who, many years later, would become a 'boy turned girl' by the name of Lily Savage!

The visits to the communal air raid shelters continued on a nightly basis and despite the pangs of fear each time the cacophony of wailing sirens warned us of the approaching enemy bombers, the trek to and from these havens of safety became almost common place. It was not unusual for us to spend three of four hours huddled together listening to the sound of carnage being inflicted above our heads but, before long, the bulldog spirit that so typified the British – and especially those born within sight of the Liver Building – began to show through and sing songs were organised. Surprisingly, in view of the career I was to follow in later life, I had no ambition to be either a singer or performer in any way – indeed my ambition for as long as I could remember and in keeping with so many other girls of the same age, was to be a nurse. I even went as far as enrolling at the local General Hospital as an Auxilliary on reaching the school leaving age of 16, but the glamorous role of the duties I had envisaged, passed me by. I spent the days cleaning out bed pans, and washing the bums of many of the hospitals elderly male patients. When I said I wanted to start at the bottom, they must have taken me literally! Everything was fine though, until I caught sight of the bloodier side of the profession and I found myself being rushed to the Accident and Emergency ward and put into intensive care on a diet of tranquillisers and water. I realised then, that I was not cut out for the job! When the opportunity arose to sing, therefore, I was first to volunteer my services. The song I sang night after night was "When They Sound The Last All Clear" in the childish hope that my rendition would actually drown out the sounds of the bombs and hopefully stop the grown ups from being scared. It was the logical reasoning of a child – if only life were that simple! The fact was, however, that I had now faced an audience for the very first time and despite an inborn shyness, found I actually enjoyed the experience.

It was a happy day when news finally came through that we had been re-housed and although we only moved two doors down from Auntie May, we had at least broken away from her sadistic ways. Our new home bore little resemblance to what we had so dearly loved whilst staying with my lovely Nan but at least it was our own. Whatever the shortcomings in its structure, Mum looked after it like a palace. Having been in service in her younger days, she knew all about the good things in life and ran the house accordingly. Whereas other households made do with newspapers, we always had a pristine tablecloth on the table and everything on show sparkled in cleanliness. She did, however, go just a little over the top when it came to the necessity of bodily functions. Once again, we suffered the indignity of an outside toilet and to alleviate the awful trudge down the steep steps in the yard to the pathway that led to instant relief, Mum had agreed that a potty could be stored under the bed – especially in the winter months when snow and ice made the freezing passage to the loo a nightmare. The trouble was though, the use of this container was strictly limited to those wishing only to pee and anyone subject to a more urgent call of nature was banished to the bitter cold of the little shed at the bottom of the yard without sympathy!

Being merely a two up and two down construction, the house offered little or no privacy. We all washed in the kitchen and I can clearly remember brother John walking through one day as I was stripping down to wash and yelling "Ay Marg – there's two pieces of cotton dangling from your knickers!" and as I frantically bent over to look, he followed up with "Sorry Marg – It's yer legs!" His laughter echoed round the house but I couldn't join in – I was too embarrassed. I had to admit though, he *did* have a point. My legs were just a little thin – just like the rest of me!

Even my Dad did not escape the pain of living in such cramped conditions – or indeed, Mum's crusade for cleanliness. Each evening, he would arrive home from his work as a shipwright at Cammell-Lairds Shipyard and before entering the house, had to stay in the back yard, remove his shoes and socks and wash his feet. Once completed, his discarded socks would then be left in the bowl to soak, while he removed his overalls before being allowed into the kitchen. Despite the conditions however, we were a happy, loving family and the adversity we endured only served to bring us closer together.

By now, I was 9 years of age and when Mum suggested I take piano lessons, I was delighted! My teacher was Miss E.J.Williams, ALCM, and despite her impressive name, was tiny in stature and would never ever win any beauty prizes! Her hair style was very severe, consisting of two plaits which wound themselves around her ears like earphones. In addition, she had five giant moles adorning her face from which sprouted unsightly hairs and I must admit – I found it difficult to take my eyes away from them! She was, however, a wonderful teacher and I enjoyed every moment with her. At 1/6d a lesson it was money well spent. My only problem in keeping up my progress was the simple fact that we had no piano – so practice was impossible. Once again, my Nan came to the rescue for she had one in her new home and invited me to use it. She was living on her own at this time, for her daughter Liz had left home to join the WAAF's whilst son-in-law Ernie served in the Royal Navy (Liz and Ern returned home safely at the end of the conflict and still live in Prenton, nr. Birkenhead, to this day). On many an occasion, it meant an overnight stay but I loved being with her and playing the piano to her. Playing well meant so much to me, even then, and I remember vividly playing a piece of music that just would not sound right, I burst into tears and took my frustration out on the poor piano. "The piano's wrong!" I cried "It's not fair, the piano's wrong". Of course, the piano was *not* to blame. I found out later, after calming down, that the piece I was playing was in the key of G and those of you who understand music will have realised that every time I hit the F, I should have been playing an F sharp! It does illustrate, however, how seriously I took my music. I did then and

My Auntie Liz & Uncle Ern – still living on the Wirral today

have always done so ever since. In time, Miss Williams and I started playing piano duets together, with me playing the bass clef and we actually entered and won, a number of musical festivals.

My early education had been at the Trinity Street Primary School but the time had come to move to a higher grade. I enrolled at the Birkenhead High School for Girls and to my delight, was taken under the wing of the music teacher – a Miss Laramie. Like Miss Williams, she too, was Welsh and under her tutorship, I learned to sing in her native language – so well, in fact, I found myself entering, and sometimes winning, Welsh Music Festivals. What Miss Laramie also tried to do was teach me the King's English in an attempt to eradicate my Scouse accent. She failed dismally! One language I did excel in was French and it became one of my favourite subjects. In fact, I attained sixth form standard long before joining that particular grade. Many years later, Nick Curtis (one of the male vocalists from The Maggie Stredder Singers) and I were frequently used to produce a series of instruction tapes, teaching French to the pupils of schools in the Inner London Education Authority.

Although I practiced long and hard at the piano, I became increasingly devoted to my singing and more and more hoped that I could begin lessons. I approached my Mum on the subject and her answer was very much to the point. "You stick with the piano" she said "and if you want singing lessons – you get yourself a job and pay for them yourself. Where do you think I'd get the money from?" Of course that was impossible for I was still only thirteen and whilst still at school, had no opportunity to earn the sort of money that was required – so for the next three years I had to content myself with spending what pocket money I received on sheet music and accompanying myself on piano, singing the songs currently in the hit parade at that time. The thought of taking singing lessons, however, never left me and I vowed that as soon as I was financially able, I would find me a good teacher and enrol.

I couldn't wait for my schooldays to finish but finally they did and my priority now was to find a job. I was granted an interview in the Borough Treasurer's office at the Town Hall and to my delight, was offered a job as a Power Samas operator – a punch card system which was the forerunner to today's computer. I took to the job quickly and became highly efficient in its operation. I became so skilled, in fact, our Head Office in London 'head hunted' me and I travelled to the Capital City for an interview – alone and scared – but passed the test with flying colours and was offered a job that filled me with great excitement. To accept meant travelling the world, teaching the system to other countries and to say that I was ecstatic, would be an understatement. I couldn't wait to tell Mum and Dad, but Mum immediately put a stop to any dreams I had been building "Yer not going Marg" she said – and as usual, Dad said nothing. "Why not?" I asked, but already my heart was sinking. "'cos London's a wicked, wicked place" she replied "a city of sin and yer not going. Anyway – who'd look after yer? – so yer not goin' and that's that" and as far as I was concerned, that **was** that. I turned it down.

One of the first things I did, however, after taking the job at the Town Hall, was to look for a singing teacher and was fortunate enough to find one by the name of Tom Jones. Sadly, he was not related to the Welsh singing star (he was much too old to move his pelvis!) but he proved good for me. To begin with, I could only afford one lesson every two weeks but soon I able to increase the tuition to one every week and my voice improved accordingly. I began to enter as many talent contests as I could and to my delight, was nearly always placed in the top three. The best one I can remember was titled 'Stairway to Stardom' and was held at the local Ritz Cinema (I can still remember the manager's name – Bill Boht) and I won. The prize was to appear at the famous Shakespeare Theatre in Liverpool, for a whole week. There was no pay, mind you, but it really was one of the high spots of my life up to then, made even more special by the fact that it was the only time my relatives came to hear me sing. I was made up!

I was 'head hunted' yet again, this time by Cammel-Lairds. I was invited to organise the punch card department in their main office and be responsible for the training of eighteen girls who would be under my control. Unfortunately, Cammel-Lairds was on strike at that particular time and the only work we did therefore, was merely practice. It was a monotonous existence and to liven things up, I began bringing my record player to the office and during the lunch time break, with the help of some Bill Haley records, we had fun times dancing to this great new sound *and* I learned how to jive!! The carefree times, however, were not to last for, shortly after, the strike was called off. The work began to pour in and the girls began to resent and finally hate the extra pressure.

Not long after, a Sunday newspaper published an exposé on the low life in London and named names of those we used to call – 'dirty old men'. It told of how they would advertise in the northern press for female dancers, singers and models to work in London – only to find themselves driven into prostitution, white slave trafficking and worse. I recalled the wise words of warning my Mum had given me previously, and not for the first time, I realised how right she had been. Thanks Mum!

CHAPTER 2

I pass an audition and my life changes for ever

The defining moment that was to change the course of my life dramatically, came in the shape of an advertisement in the Liverpool Echo. It simply said "Can you sing? Female singers wanted. Famous vocal group. Write re: age, experience etc". It gave a Box No. to reply to and with Mum's advice still ringing in my ears, I viewed the situation with grave suspicion. Nevertheless, I decided to reply and concocted a letter listing all my talents and more, laying it on thick and very much tongue in cheek. "I'll show these horrible little men", I thought, and genuinely never expected to hear another word. To my surprise, an official looking letter arrived a few days later, typed on Vernons Pools headed notepaper and inviting me to audition. I was still suspicious, however, and as a safeguard for any possible foul play to come, arrived at the perfect solution – I'll take my Dad with me. He'll sort them out! We duly turned up on the day with me dressed up to the nines – probably more suited to a society wedding than audition but what-the-hell, I was determined to make an impression. I wore a powder pink coat with pearl buttons, a navy blue picture hat with matching shoes and gloves and carrying, of course, my music case! When the advert appeared there had been over 300 replies but systematically this had now been reduced to the final short list of 50 who were parading their talent this day. All shapes, all sizes and all types!

The dignitaries, or should I say 'those to he afraid of', were the formidable chaperon to the Vernons Girls – Miss Marion Finegan, the famous Musical Director from T.V and recording fame – Peter Knight, a charming, chubby, gentle little man – Tom Grenfell, Head of Publicity from Vernons Pools, Mr. Parker, the Musical Director from the Shakespeare Theatre in Liverpool and Leslie Cooper, a choreographer from London.

I watched the proceedings, feeling increasingly sick, as the numbers reduced but, at long last, the waiting was over. "Margaret   Stredder please" came the command. I walked forward. Peter Knight introduced himself. "Music please, Darling" he said and added in a whisper "Don't be afraid". It was too late – I already was. Not afraid – terrified! The piece I had chosen was 'Only Make Believe' from the musical 'Showboat' and after placing myself in the singing position, took a deep breath and started. As I moved into the song I felt my confidence returning line by line, and by the finish was actually enjoying the experience. To my delight and surprise, there was a lovely round of unexpected applause, but the mood of pleasure that had engulfed me was dispelled in an instant when, to my horror, I saw one of the 'important people' walk towards me. "Congratulations on your performance" he said "Now please lift your skirt. We'd like to see your legs!" I nearly died. I looked round in panic hoping to see the one person who could get me out of this. Where was my Dad? I had no option and lifted my skirt as decorously and neatly as I could. "Thank you" the 'important person' said "That's fine. Please sit over there".

One incident which I found very funny concerned two girls who had applied as a duo – not the norm and certainly most unusual. They were dressed as 'Teddy' girls, wearing tightly tapered black skirts, split up the back and on their feet, flat black pumps. Their hair was greased down and they both sported D.A'.s. As he had done with me, Peter Knight politely asked them for their music.

"Haven't got none" they replied in fluent Scouse.

"What are you going to sing?" persisted Mr. Knight

"'Dream' by The Everley Brothers," they replied, but Peter, refusing to be fazed, persevered.

"What key do you sing it in?" he continued

"What's that?" was the answer "What's a key. Don't know nuttin about that. You just start playin' and we'll join in!"

Peter started to play. "No – too high. Down – no, too low – up again". Eventually, however, the problems were sorted and to everyone's surprise they were great – two female Everley Brothers doing their thing. Who'd have thought?

Finally, the moment of truth and it was announced that five girls in all had been selected to join the group – Helen Taylor, Betty Liddy, Mary Redmond & Ann O'Brien (the two Everley brothers!!) and me. I was so thrilled and it was lovely to realise too, that all five selected came from 'over the water' – Birkenhead. We bonded immediately. In fact Ann, with the tight skirt, pumps and DA, is my very best friend to this day and she was later to join me as a very hard working member of the Ladybirds.   I love her and   admire her greatly.

The Vernons Girls, which we were now about to join, was formed in 1953 as part of the social activities of Vernons Pools and began, originally as a 30 strong choir chosen from within the Company's female work force, performing mainly for charity. So popular did they become however, they decided to turn professional three years later, appearing in variety and summer season shows. By now, they had reduced in number to 16 girls and when five of the group were sacked for behaviour unbefitting a Vernons Girl, it was decided to audition for 'outside talent'. I was one of the five to be chosen and I could not believe my good fortune. I refused, however, to get carried away until I had negotiated the final stumbling block – Mum and Dad, but to my amazement and joy they agreed I could accept the offer "because I would be heavily chaperoned!" I was so thrilled and couldn't wait for the first day to arrive and when it did, I entered the doors of the Bluecoat Chambers in Liverpool, flushed with excitement. The great adventure was about to begin!!

The Legendary Vernons Girls, 1957

19

CHAPTER 3

It's hard work being a Vernons Girl!

We had been asked to wear loose fitting clothes as rehearsal gear for the first day and we entered the allocated room excited yet just a little apprehensive, not knowing quite what to expect. In addition, the existing members of the group eyed the five newcomers with suspicion and maybe even a touch of resentment, for were we not taking the places of friends and colleagues whom they had been with for some time? It was natural and understandable but it caused a slight air of tension until we got to know them better. Thankfully, that didn't take long and with our love of music and particularly singing as the catalyst, we soon began to make friends.

Miss Finegan sprang the first surprise of the day, however, by producing a giant jar of Arid cream deodorant. She stood in front of us, like an officer taking the salute, with the open jar held out before her and we, in turn lined up in single file and as we passed the proffered container, we scooped an appropriate amount with our fingers and dabbed it under our armpits, as she looked on. I know it was 1957 but I really did feel that most people knew about, and were using, deodorants – but apparently not! Our first lesson was now over and we took comfort from the fact that no Vernons Girl at least, would warrant an upturned nose or a painful sniff in any crowded room. Miss Finegan had been a Sergeant Major in the Territorial Army and had probably come across some smelly girls before and this obviously prompted her to ensure that whatever we lacked in vocal and dance talent – we would always smell nice!

The choreographer, Leslie Cooper, travelled from London for two and a half days every week to put us through our paces. He was a handsome man with quite the longest eyelashes I have ever seen and as well as being a brilliant dancer, was a superb tutor. He worked us very, very hard but – oh – how it paid off! Realising that not one of us had had any kind of formal training, (we could barely put one foot in front of the other), he devised and choreographed routines which resulted in us becoming a 16 strong, finely tuned dance troupe with the precision of military guardsmen. The training I received from Leslie Cooper in these early days with the Vernons girls, has stayed with me throughout my entire professional career and I know, too, that every other girl who shared the same formal coaching will wholeheartedly agree with me when I say – thank you, Leslie.

Although dancing was a major part of the course, he also taught us how to walk, move, stand and pose. He would start off each day by arranging us into 'height lines' – tallest on the right, shortest on the left – and it was easy for me, being 5' 8" and the tallest, to take up my position. Staying in the lines, he would make us walk, stand still, pose, sit with legs crossed, legs uncrossed, stand up and turn. We would do it time after time after time until we could perform it to his satisfaction; We did simple barre work, learning the ballet position before progressing to doing spins across the room This involved pin pointing a spot diagonally on the far side of the floor, spinning around quickly, remembering to bring the head around last and fixing our eyes firmly on the chosen spot. More often than not, we ended up all over the place, in the wrong direction and invariably, in a heap on the floor! Again however, we improved with hard work and dedication and soon we were performing the steps, spins and movements with ease.

The other two and a half days per week were devoted to music and were coached by the lovely, gentle Mr. Parker from the Shakespeare Theatre in Liverpool. He would divide us into 3 sections – sopranos, mezzo-sopranos and contraltos – and teach us the harmonies for each group. Finally the three sections would sing all at the same time and the resultant sound was magic. My knowledge of the theory of music gained from my piano lessons, was invaluable and I enjoyed helping the others, especially our special group of the five newcomers (from across the water). At the end of each day when we arrived back at Birkenhead Station, we would settle around a table at Olivieri's, a local coffee bar, and I would go over the music we had to learn and try explain to them the bits that were proving difficult in a way they were able to understand. Ann, particularly, responded to this extra help for she had then, and still has to this day, an unquenchable thirst for knowledge.

The days flew by and we loved every moment of the training we were being given but, understandably, longed for the moment when we would perform for real. It was not long in coming and we were over the moon when we learned it was to be on the TV hit show 'Six-five Special'. The music for the show was decided and we redoubled our efforts with Mr. Parker to learn the melodies and harmonies that were required. I was given a one-line solo – "I'm all shook up!" – and I nearly died at the thought, bearing in mind that in the past, I had only ever sung classical or 'very naice' songs from the shows in public. However, as the routine was an Elvis Presley medley, I realised I had little or no choice – and that, very firmly, was that! We were told, too, that some of us (the tall, thin ones) would be wearing shorts, tights and high heels plus tops, (I hasten to add), with the rest in dresses. Imagine the laugh we had when we discovered that Mary and Ann (the Everley Bros) were to wear shorts with the words ELVIS and PRESLEY printed on their bums! This meant that, in effect, only their posteriors would be seen on the screen along with my face as I belted out "I'm all shook up!" and wiggled my boobs in tempo. At least I can say, unlike the other two, that *my* TV career didn't start at the bottom! As crude as this sequence sounds, it actually worked wonderfully well thanks, once again, to some clever choreography by Leslie Cooper. Gosh he was good!

The excitement built and the day finally arrived when we had to travel to London for the show. We all met on the platform at Lime Street Station in Liverpool and we could barely contain our composure. We piled into our reserved compartment with our cardboard suitcases in tow and waved good-bye to our Mums and Dads who lined the platform to see us off. Amidst the thrill of what we were about to do, was a feeling of apprehension for this really was my first time away from home on my own. And let's face it – like it or not, I was now in the big time!!

We arrived at Euston Station and piled into taxis that took us to our reserved accommodation – The Colonnade Hotel in Maida Vale. It was run by the Richards family and is still there to this day, still a family business but now, thanks to continued investment, very, very beautiful and 'up market'. Maybe the fact that the Vernons Girls once stayed there helped them on their way! The bedrooms were enormous – they had to be as we were sharing four to a room! One of the girls I shared with was Barbara, the Head Girl, who'd been with the group since it was formed in 1953. She had gained a reputation for giving us 'withering' looks if we were naughty – but I later found out that the glare she scared us half to death with, was not a show of disapproval as we had imagined, but severe myopia! We became firm friends then – and still are today. The other girls with me were little Betty, a delicate pocket Venus with a great sense of humour and Helen, the only married woman in the group, who had stunning good looks and legs that seemed to on for ever. Sadly, today the legs that demanded so much attention, now give her much suffering.

The day dawned – our first day of real rehearsals for our very first real TV show. We met up in the reception hall at 8.00 am and lined up for inspection. Barbara was responsible for getting us to that point on time but such was the excitement, we would have made it easily under our own steam. From then onwards, however, Barbara's task would be made that much harder by two of the girls – Lyn & Jean – who took the art of being late for everything to professional standards! Once in line, Miss Finegan looked us over, intent, as always, on missing nothing. No ladders, no headscarfs. Were we wearing *clean* white gloves? Had our lipstick been applied tastefully? Was our hair looking good? Did we have a brolly, in case it rained? She looked us over with a fine toothcomb and only when she was totally satisfied did she let us leave the hotel. Even then, we had to leave in crocodile formation in our now familiar, height line with Miss Finegan at the helm. We came to cross the main road, heavy with the morning rush hour traffic, and she fearlessly strode out into its midst, raised her hand and, oblivious to the screeching of brakes and the yelling of irate drivers, shouted "Forward girls" and we did. Yes honestly! I tell you, the first time she did this, we nearly died. Anyway, there was this bevy of young beauties travelling across London to TV stardom, riding on public transport. It was hysterical! The fact that the mode of transport continued even after we had become famous, made it even funnier. It wouldn't happen today! We arrived at the studio still looking and feeling in pristine condition, to be met by Pete Murray, Freddie Mills, Josephine Douglas and Don Lang (of the Frantic Five) – the resident presenters of the show. The guest of that particular show was a handsome but pimply faced and very nervous singer making his television debut and from that raw but successful beginning, emerged one of the great pop vocalists of the era – Adam Faith. We were to back Adam as well as performing our own numbers, in addition to 'dressing' the set and, without doubt, it was to be one of the very best days of my life.

CHAPTER 4

It's 'The Six Five Special'

I wanted to remember every moment of that wonderful day and I can recall whispering to a colleague "my singing teacher will drop dead when he sees what I'm doing". Sadly my words, said in jest, proved prophetic for two months later, he did just that and I can only hope that the sight of me on TV singing 'I'm all shook up' and wiggling my boobs had nothing to do with it! Throughout the day we rehearsed non stop and even when the producer called 'tea break everyone – take 15'. Leslie Cooper would shout 'except the Vernons Girls' and we would continue working to keep polishing what was already a highly polished presentation. The show came and went in what seemed minutes. The transmission in those days was live but there was no time to feel nervous – in any event, we knew the routines so well by now, we could have done them in our sleep. In all we did another four shows in the 'Six-Five Special' series and by now we were beginning to create a huge impression with the viewing public. Our trademark was one of punctuality (despite Jean & Lyn), professionalism, good bearing, cleanliness, neatness and sheer class. After all, we were told time and time again, we were the ambassadors for Vernons Pools and we certainly took this responsibility very seriously. If we hadn't, there is little doubt we would have been shown the door and that would have been a disaster too great to contemplate.

Occasionally we found ourselves involved in not one, but two different shows running at the same time – the aforementioned 'Six-five Special' and, in contrast, a show called 'New Look'. This made stars out of many of the regulars who appeared in it, Bruce Forsyth, Roy Castle, Des O'Connor (fresh from his 'redcoat' duties at Butlin's), Jack Douglas and Joe Baker plus a dancing brother and sister act, Lionel and Joyce Blair. They were great to do – not rock'n'roll but lovely *real* singing and *real* dancing and we wore elegant dresses. We were partnered by real professional TV 'male' dancers. (I've put the work 'male' in inverted commas because of the lingering doubt I had over their sexuality – common place today but a novelty to us somewhat naïve young ladies at that time). They were fabulous fun to work with and they helped us enormously. They, in turn, thoroughly enjoyed working with the 16 'green' Scousers who looked good but talked funny!

I mentioned how naïve we were and this characteristic was fully exploited on the day we arrived for our very first day of rehearsal. We were young, impressionable and couldn't wait to meet the stars of the show – no different to anyone else comparatively new to the business. To our disappointment, there was no sign of any of the big names and we felt a sense of anti-climax. The Director of the show, anxious to get things moving, pointed his finger at us.

"You –you – you – and you" he yelled (and I was one of the 'you's') rehearsal room 2 and look over your lines". He handed us our scripts and off we went to start work. We found the allocated room, and without a thought, barged in. We stopped dead in our tracks for there, like a scene from the movie 'The Full Monty' stood the stars we were so anxious to meet, totally naked except for the briefest of briefs. There they were in all their glory – Bruce Forsyth, Roy Castle, Des O'Connor, Lionel Blair, Jack Douglas and Joe Baker! Like the troupers they undoubtedly were, they never turned a hair but merely waved and called a greeting 'Morning girls!' And like the immature greenhorns that we were, we gasped, threw our hands in the air – and fled to seek urgent counselling. We were shocked to the core. Let's face it, I had never, ever seen a pair of men's underpants before, unless you count the ones which belonged to my Dad and which Mum used to hang out on the washing line – but they don't really count because they were, in fact, long john's! It took us days to recover and even the explanation that they had simply been there for costume fitting, failed to ease the shock. Today, of course, we look back and laugh at how silly we were. Bruce and I keep up the gag. Each time we meet, I will pretend not to have met him before and say to him "Bruce Forsyth! – I didn't recognise you with your clothes on!" and he in turn will say "Hi Maggie. How are you off for Valium?" Happy days!

With the 'Six-Five Special' coming to the end of its natural life, the idea to send the show on tour around theatres in the UK was proposed and approved. Featured on stage were the resident presenters – Pete Murray, Freddie Mills and Josephine Douglas with Don Lang & the Frantic Five, The Vernons Girls and Adam Faith. It was a whirlwind tour in the true sense of the word and one town merged into another. It was simply a case of – all on the coach – all off the coach – perform the show – back to

John & Cissie Stredder – my dearest Mum & Dad

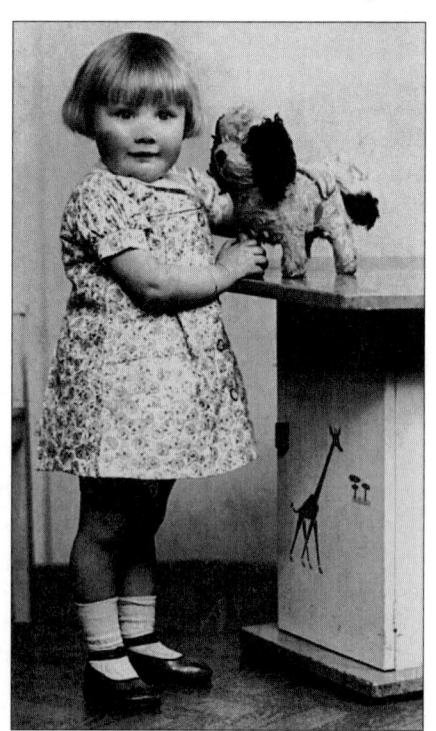

Me – aged 3, and showing half a knicker (money-conscious even then!)

*Adam Faith –
and not a pimple in sight*

*Marty – 'mean and moody' –
with the Vernons Girls*

*Four legends of pop
(L to R) Marty Wilde,
Cliff Richard, Jack Good &
Joe Brown*

*Two guys & a gal!
Conway Twitty, Marty Wilde &
me on 'Oh Boy'*

*'C'mon, everybody'
– meet Eddie Cochran*

*On the 'Oh Boy' show, live with
Billy Fury*

Gene Vincent makes an impression on the Girls

Making a Pathé Pictorial film with Jack Good

the Hotel – early call – all on the coach again – and so begins another day! It was tiring, it was exhausting, but it was exciting and it was fun. It was also a great learning experience and we found that the discipline of being on the road and in the theatre was so different to that of the studio. Miss Finegan, of course, travelled with us and, as always, ruled with a rod of iron. From the day of joining the Vernons Girls, she had devised a set of rules that were laid in stone – particularly when recording in London and staying at the Colonnade Hotel. They went as follows:

- No boyfriends
- Never go out alone, minimum of two
- In bed by 11 p.m.
- Inform Miss Finegan if going out
- No smoking whilst working or in the street.
- No going out the evening before TV show

If anyone imagined that the lovely girls they watched week after week on television led lives filled with sex, drugs and rock'n'roll, then perhaps they can think again. The life was glamorous and we loved every minute of it but off stage, we lived an existence akin to a nunnery – and that, I guess, was what persuaded my Mum and Dad to let me join! Deep down, however, although we outwardly agreed with the restrictions, we resented being treated like children and occasionally 'bent' the rules. It was not a case of being deliberately naughty or evil. – more a case of rebellion instigated to relieve boredom. It was my birthday and to help us celebrate, we smuggled some male companions in to share the occasion; there was nothing sinister planned, it was all innocent and above board, but we knew we were out of bounds and the very feeling of danger added spice to the event. In another room lay one of our colleagues by the name of Peggy, suffering from the 'flu and to our dismay we heard Miss Finegan passing our door to visit the stricken girl. We moved like lightning and if she had chosen to look in, would have seen four girls sleeping the sleep of the innocent. Had she looked under the bed however, she would have seen four trembling, terrified males fervently praying for mercy.

On another occasion, one Friday (pay night) a few of us sneaked out to the local pub. We were not drinkers by any stretch of the imagination, but were in a devilish mood. It was the evening before a TV show and the Finegan rule was that we should all be locked away in our rooms. Of course, the 'iron lady' found out and went ballistic! Maybe this was the straw that broke the camel's back but, brave little me, I decided to write to

Tom Grenfell from Vernons Pools and acquaint him of the rules and regulations that bound us. He met with us all the next time we were in Liverpool and, to our delight, announced that from this day onwards we would have our freedom. We could smoke if we wished – and to illustrate the point threw a packet of cigarettes into our midst – and the rules that governed our very movements away from home would be relaxed. As if with one pair of eyes we turned to Miss Finegan. Her face was like thunder and she glared at each of us in turn as we lit up. Tom continued "You can now go out as you wish. You may also go out with men but let me tell you" he paused dramatically to emphasise the point "Any bad publicity or anyone getting pregnant – the group will be disbanded immediately. You have been warned!"

From that moment on, we started to lead a more normal existence but I hesitate to use the word 'happier' for the Colonnade Hotel became more commonly known as the Heartbreak Hotel because of the number of female hearts that were broken within its four walls. Maybe Miss Finegan was right after all!

My 'official' fan club photograph

CHAPTER 5

Two Weddings & the 'Oh Boy' Show

The moment that was to change my life for ever came with the announcement of the 'Oh Boy' show from Jack Good. It was 1958 and for the first time ever a rock'n'roll show was to regularly hit the TV screens devoid of silly jokes and tired comedy routines. It was music all the way and featured the very best artistes from both sides of the Atlantic with back up music from the John Barry Seven and Lord Rockinghams XI. The show was compered by Jimmy Henney and Tony Hall, overall direction was by Rita Gillespie and it was presented on the stage of the Hackney Empire before a live audience of 250 rock'n'roll fans. The atmosphere was unlike anything else on British TV and even in America, there was nothing to compete with it. The average weekly TV audience was in excess of 10 million and it was a total smash. The fan mail poured in and my fears of being relegated to the back row and oblivion went in the opposite direction. I was featured in everything – and not just in the show. Newspaper interviews, photographed by the press constantly and I was amazingly featured on the front cover of 'Woman's Weekly'. They even filmed me for a Pathé Pictorial Newsreel called 'Specs for Showgirls' which played in all the major cinemas throughout the UK. I was given my own personal copy, years later, which had been transferred to video but I cannot watch it without suffering acute embarrassment! Nevertheless, it projected me into celebrity status and it was very flattering but equally disconcerting to walk on stage at the 'Oh Boy' show and be faced with dozens of 'Maggie Stredder' clones sitting in the audience complete with blonde 'cottage loaf' hairstyles and black-rimmed glasses. I couldn't believe it was happening to me – but it was and I allowed myself to wallow in the excitement. Offers came in to join this group or that group and even to go solo but I wasn't interested. I felt safe and secure within the Vernons Girls and no one could get to me. I was being cared for and protected and the wolves that infect our business were being kept at bay –

and all because Jack Good had insisted I wear my glasses! As a footnote, the sale of specs throughout Great Britain rose to an unprecedented high – and *I* got the credit. Thousands of impressionable young women began to believe, at long last, that guys *do* make passes at gals who wear glasses!

His unerring eye for a gimmick, however, didn't just stop with me. You will recall my tale of the two young ladies of 'Everley Brothers' fame and, nice to relate, they too had become hits by re-creating the boys in an Everley Brothers routine. One day Ann (one half of the duo) turned up for the show sporting a very bad and painful stye on her eye, feeling sure that Jack would take out the number. No possible way! He instructed her to wear an eye patch (covered with sequins of course) and she too became a sensation, receiving fan mail by the sack load!

Yet another performer projected to fame by the Jack Good genius for a gimmick was the American Gene Vincent. Gene had suffered from polio since childhood and wore a special boot but did all in his power to hide the deformity – until he met Jack. Instead of concealing the unsightly footwear, Good determined to feature it and whilst Vincent was performing and the show was going out live, he would crawl under the camera, shouting loud enough for only the singer to hear "The boot, Gene, – the boot – don't forget to drag the boot, let the viewers see the boot!"

As well as his skill in spotting gimmicks, Jack Good was a brilliant spotter of talent. He auditioned a nervous and very inexperienced young man by the name of Cliff Richard and immediately gave him a slot in the show. He also booked Cliff's group, The Drifters (who later changed their name to the Shadows to avoid confusion with the American vocal group) and they did extremely well. Cliff and the Drifters were so anxious, however, to do another show, that they hung around the rehearsal rooms day after day, so that Jack wouldn't forget them. We (The Vernons Girls) would breakfast at a nearby coffee bar with the boys and one day they told us that they had spent the night in a Turkish Bath in Marylebone as they had no money left for digs. At that time we were only earning £7.00 a week each (with £3.00 of that being sent home) but often had enough left to buy them coffee and toast. It really was that bad! I remember, too, one deep conversation I had with The Shadows, whilst doing their second 'Oh Boy' show. We were sitting on the stairs behind the set at the Hackney Empire and I offered them advice which haunts me to this day. "If you really stick at it and practice very hard" I said "You could be very good!" How embarrassing! They never fail to remind me when I see them. That one goes into the file marked "Things I wish I hadn't said".

Other stars featured regularly on the show and amongst the most popular, was Marty Wilde. He was such a lovely boy to know and I have to say that the stardom he so rightly achieved has never changed him. He is still the same delightful man with no side to him in any way and not the slightest hint of conceit. At that time he had his eyes on sweet pretty Sybil – one of our girls – and she, in turn, liked him too. Mind you – we all did! Ever the gentleman, he asked Miss Finegan if he could take her to dinner (remember the rules?) and she agreed. A date was arranged to their mutual delight. Sadly, on the day, Sybil was struck down with 'flu and instead, Marty took out the youngest and most recent Vernons Girl – Joyce. They fell in love and on the 2nd December 1959 they married at the Christ Church in Greenwich, East London, with the reception arranged at the fabulous showbiz Chinese Restaurant "The Lotus House" in the Edgeware Road.

Joyce, so young and pretty, looked just like a story-book fairy princess. The bridesmaids – Barbara Mitchell, Lyn Cornell, Betty Prescott and our only married Vernons Girl, Helen Taylor – were stunning in beautiful peach dresses but, such was the cold on the big day, each commented that white fox stoles would have been a more acceptable addition to the outfit! The rest of us spent the time fussing and clucking around them like mother hens – primping and preening and tweaking, whether it needed it or not but with every good reason for today was the day our 'baby' of the group was to marry and we wanted it to be perfect. And so it was! They have now been married for over 40 years raising four beautiful children – the most well known being Kim (Wilde) who presented them with a grandson Harry Tristan – a little Capricorn (just like me!) and a little beauty – Rose Elizabeth.

After the astonishing success of the 'Oh Boy' series, Jack Good wanted to showcase his genius yet again and devised a format based on similar lines to 'Oh Boy' but much gentler and slower in pace. He called it 'Boy Meets Girls'. It lacked the frenetic pace of its predecessor, as well as its impact but, nevertheless (and surprisingly) it was very well received by the viewing public.

It featured many of those who had been seen before but, in true Jack Good style, introduced many newcomers who, like those preceding, would reach stardom.

One such person was a cheeky chappie with a Cockney accent you could cut with a knife, spiky hair and an ear to ear grin that warmed every front room in the country. His name was Joe Brown and, in

Wedding Belles (1) ... Our Joyce marries pop star – Marty Wilde
(Photograph courtesy of Marty Wilde)

Wedding Belles (2) ... Our Vicky marries pop star – Joe Brown, without the disguise

addition to possessing a good voice, played guitar (plus a number of other stringed instruments including mandolin and banjo) quite brilliantly. The fact that he had a wickedly funny sense of humour was the icing on the cake and endeared him to audiences everywhere he appeared. Today he is still in demand, is still greatly loved and has changed very little, both physically and by nature. In true romantic fashion and living up to the title of the show – boy **met** girl. The boy was Joe and the girl was our very own darling Vicky.

With Joe around, there were always lots of gags, loads of kidology and we never stopped laughing! In the early days of the romance, whilst we were staying, yet again, at the famous Colonnade Hotel in London, Vicky smuggled Joe into the room she now shared with Barbara, Betty and I. The room was at the top of the stairs, guarded by one of our look-outs who would warn us of the impending arrival of Miss Finegan. Suddenly there was a frantic knocking on our door with the warning "Miss Finegan on the hunt!" Joe was trapped and his only escape route was through the window. He found, however, it was too high to jump so he hung there by his fingertips with his legs dangling into space, until the danger had passed and we were able to drag him back in. It must have looked hysterical to those passing by on the main road outside, for the Hotel was floodlit!! Joe's constant flow of one liners kept us in stitches, especially his pet nickname for our 'tallest on the right, shortest on the left' crocodile formation that Miss Finegan loved to lead. "Here it comes" Joe would say "the bloody crumpet train!"

By now their romance was serious, they were very much in love and a few years later on the 10th December 1963 they married. Not everyone was happy, however, for Joe's manager bitterly opposed the union, working on the theory that his highly successful attempt to project Joe as a sex symbol to his army of fans could blow up in his face and ruin his career overnight. He found, however, that Cupid's arrow was too deeply embedded in the hearts of the love birds and conceding the fact he could do little to prevent the nuptial, went to enormous lengths to prevent anyone actually finding out. He allowed the guests to take their cameras but would not allow them to use film and – worst of all – took *us* off the invitation list. Sixteen beautiful recognisable young ladies, he reasoned, would surely alert the ever prowling press. The whole event was shrouded in secrecy and to Joe – well this was right up his wicked street and played right into his hands. Vicky, of course, was radiant – so, so beautiful and looking every inch a creation made in Hollywood. Joe, too, could have come from the film capital but more likened to a Max Sennett comedy character for he decided to support his managers fears and wore a disguise – choosing a hideous black wig and heavy rimmed glasses. The effect when he entered the church was one of pure farce. Joe's brother-in-law (to be) Neil, swears to this day that the red weals on his knuckles were caused by ramming his fist into his mouth to prevent his whole being from collapsing into hysterics. Joe, being Joe, didn't see it as being at all funny. "I looked great" he said "but I was still scared I would get mobbed 'cos when I looked into the mirror – I looked the bloody image of Cliff Richard!" Only Joe could have got away with that!

The marriage of Vicky and Joe was very much part of a set of coincidences and similarities that linked the Cockney singer with his fellow star and very close friend, Marty Wilde. To list them, shows what an uncanny and amazing path their careers both on and off the stage have led. To begin with Joe's first date with Vicky was to attend Marty's wedding to Joyce, four years earlier. Both, of course, married Vernons Girls and both sired famous singing daughters – Marty with Kim (Wilde) and Joe with Sam (Brown). Both had sons who became record producers – Ricky, the son of Marty and Pete the son of Joe and both stars are now grandfathers. The only comparison, not chronicled, however, is pointed out by Joe. "I was always better looking!" he says simply.

Sadly, however, the coincidences end there for Marty's was a happy long lasting marriage whilst Joe's was to end tragically with the death of Vicky at the comparatively early age of 50, from cancer. She was a stunning looking girl – as beautiful within as she was on the outside and is sorely missed by everyone who came in contact with her. She was a young lady with a superb singing voice and shortly after leaving the Vernons Girls, was to start a vocal backing group called The Breakways with two other Vernons Girls, Betty Prescott and Margot Quantrell (at the same time that I formed the Ladybirds). A year before she was taken ill, stardom, as a solo artiste, came her way in Holland and big things were beginning to happen but, sadly, she never lived to enjoy the success her talent so richly deserved.

Dear Vicky – now gone but never forgotten.

CHAPTER 6

I get the sack – for four hours!

The Vernons Girls' agent during this period of time was a small Jewish man by the name of Stanley Barnet. He wore glasses, a trilby hat and from his mouth jutted a large cigar which seemed to live there permanently – in short, he was the archetypal theatrical agent. We were not his only clients, however, and like every good agent (and in fairness, he was!) he gave the acts he managed, his personal support by travelling to the venue he had booked for them and watching them perform.

This was the reason, therefore, that he found himself travelling to Germany to view, at first hand, a number of acts he had booked to tour the US Army bases throughout the country. During one show he attended, one of his American hosts, after finding out the job he did and the reason he was there, asked him if he would care to meet a young soldier on the base who 'played some guitar and sang a bit' Stanley not wishing to offend agreed and found himself being introduced to a tall, good looking G.I. by the name of Elvis Presley! Elvis was delightful to talk to and was intrigued when he found that Stanley had a strong connection with the 'Oh Boy Show'. "I hear the show is fantastic" Elvis said "one of the greatest rock'n'roll shows on TV. My good friend Johnny Cash has done the gig and can't stop raving about it". Not realising that Stanley managed us, he then went on to say the words that were to be, perhaps, the greatest compliment we have ever been paid – bearing in mind the person who said it! "And I un'erstand you have some swingin' gals in the show that are just sensational!" Wow! Like us, when we heard the story later, Stanley rose to twice his normal height with pride (even then, he didn't come up to the Elvis shoulder) and told him that everything he had heard was true (what an agent!) and like the business man he undoubtedly was – and sensing a healthy commission – he said to the King of rock'n'roll "Why don't you fly to England, Elvis, and we'll put you on the show". Elvis paused for a moment as if tempted "Sorry man" he eventually replied "It just won't happen. I'm under contract to Uncle Sam!" What a great shame – what a great pity! What a show that would have been. Elvis and the Vernons Girls. How would that have looked on *his* C.V.? Sensational!

For all Stanley's pride in us however, it must be said that this was the agent who actually sacked Barbara, Jean and me from the Vernons Girls – if only for four hours! The story of that momentous decision started when Stanley rang us to say that the great Bernard Delfont had been in touch with him, asking for three of the group to possibly appear in his summer season show at the London Palladium. It was perfect timing, for the 'Oh Boy' series had just finished its run for the time being and we were temporarily out of work. The selected trio (Barbara, Jean and I) were to audition for the great man and with Vernons Pools blessing plus the help of Leslie Cooper the choreographer, we rehearsed hard and on the appointed day arrived at the Palladium ready to impress. Impress we certainly did and when all the nice things had been said and done, we left Stanley and Bernard Delfont to sort out the business details.

We were distraught to find on our return, after a celebratory lunch, that Stanley Barnet had cancelled the deal for the one main reason that Mr. Delfont, who incidentally loved our act, would not hear of us being called the Vernons Girls and wanted to call us by our Christian names – simply 'Barbara, Jean & Maggie'. As we were still under contract to Vernons Pools, however, it was obvious that they wouldn't hear of this – so Stanley had pulled the plug. It was a devastating blow for the money we had been offered far exceeded what we were currently earning. The V.Gs were on a regular weekly wage of £9 whether we were working away or resting back home. Not really very much but probably the average weekly wage in those days. However, all our hotels, food and other expenses whilst away were met by Vernons Pools. In addition, the chance to work a summer season at the London Palladium was everyone's dream – so we argued and argued again. Barbara and I were prepared to see both sides, but Jean, always the vociferous one and certainly the most fiery, ploughed on. Tempers became heated but still Jean wouldn't let go until finally Stanley snapped. "That's it!" he yelled "I've had all I can take. Get out – you're sacked!"

We retired to a nearby hotel lounge to take stock of what had just transpired and the good news was, that now we had been flung out of the Vernons Girls, we could actually do the season at the Palladium and I rang an old friend and agent – Peter Charlesworth (who was later to handle my career when I became one of the 'Two Tones') and he readily agreed to conclude the deal on our behalf. In the meantime the phones between London and Liverpool were red hot and it was not long before Tom Grenfell from Vernons actually tracked us down. He asked for Barbara – rightly so for she was (or had been) Head Girl. "What are you doing" he said "of course you're not sacked. Meet me tomorrow at Stanley's office and we'll sort the whole thing out". We agreed and Tom apparently jumped on the first train south and was there when we appeared the following day. His pleadings continued unabated and we found ourselves weakening. He pointed out how invaluable we were to the group (his words, I assure you!) and if we left, the whole group would break up and although we knew perfectly well that *no-one* was irreplaceable, it was still flattering to hear. Anyway – eventually he wore us all down and we finally agreed to forget the trio, forget the London Palladium and forget our expulsion – we were re-instated and life retuned to normal. I still wonder, however, what may have happened if we had stuck to our guns and gone our own way. Maybe this book would have had a different ending. We will never know!

CHAPTER 7

Our first Royal Variety Show and the end of the Vernons Girls

It was an era of great excitement for us all. No sooner had we finished one series of TV shows and another would be offered to us. I was in constant demand both with the Vernons Girls and as 'Maggie Stredder' and time seemed to fly by. If I had been thrilled by the work I was doing and the stars I was now meeting,   the biggest thrill of all was to come in May 1960. The Vernons Girls were invited to appear in the Royal Variety Show at the Victoria Palace in London, in the presence of Her Majesty, The Queen and H.R.H. The Duke of Edinburgh.

I felt sure I was dreaming! Me – the skinny kid from Birkenhead – the waif who lived in Hope Street with its crumbling houses and damp rotting walls. Me – the undernourished urchin who sang for the frightened souls in an air-raid shelter hoping her thin childish voice would drown out the sounds of the German bombers and the exploding bombs. And now, years later, I was to appear in London before the Queen of the Land. It was a fairy story but one which came true.

We had no time to feel nervous. Leslie Cooper rehearsed us like never before and if we thought he had been strict in the past – then we were forced to think again. He put the fear of God into us!

"One foot wrong" he roared "one foot wrong or one hand out of place and you're out – sacked – immediately!" Talk about scared. He ruled us with tactics of terror. But you know something? We survived, every one of us and we lived to tell the tale – and what a wonderful glittering tale it was. It was a night to remember, a night in which we took our place in a galaxy of stars, a Royal feast of variety – a glorious dish to set before the Queen.

Our part of the show, compered by the man with the sexy underpants, Bruce Forsyth, was to appear in a section called 'Focus on Youth' (in effect, a carbon copy of the 'Oh Boy' show). Appearing with us was Lonnie Donegan and his Group, the John Barry Seven (which included

Dennis King ex King Brothers and the brilliant pianist/songwriter Les Reed) Adam Faith and Cliff Richard and the Shadows (Jet Harris, Hank Marvin. Tony Meehan and Bruce Welch). The 20 minute routine was produced, of course, by Jack Good and we were cheered to the echo. Of course, I was delighted at our reception but in some ways it was secondary to the thrill of mixing and mingling with so many fantastic stars – some who I'd only heard on record or seen at the Gaumont Cinema in Birkenhead. Let me list the names of those who appeared on that glittering evening – and if anyone says I'm making this up, I've still got the programmes to prove it!

From America came Liberace, Sammy Davis Jnr. Nat King Cole and Robert Horton (the handsome actor from the TV western "Wagon Train") and the best of British included (and I've even had to cut some names out to save space) Max Bygraves, Vera Lynn, The Crazy Gang, Benny Hill, Bob Monkhouse, Norman Wisdom, Harry Worth, Billy Cotton and his Band, Russ Conway, Ivor Emmanuel, Ronnie Hilton, Alma Cogan, Anne Shelton and many more – all household names. It was the thirty first Royal Variety Performance (the first was in March 1921) and surely this must have been the very best – or am I just a little biased?

We were, of course, introduced to the Royal Party at the end of the show but like many others before me and equally many after, I cannot recall the handshake or what (if anything) was said – as hard as I try. Everything in my memory is simply a blur but a very happy one, nonetheless. In actual fact, we were invited to appear in a further nine Royal Variety Shows, mostly as backing singers to star vocalists (and known, by then, as the Ladybirds) and I would like to think that this is some sort of record, particularly for singers! I will, however, never forget the first. It holds a very special place in my heart.

Despite the unqualified success of 'Boy Meets Girls', Jack Good was restless and becoming bored with its laid back formula and it was no surprise to any of us when he produced a new concept to be called 'Wham'. It was an in-between kind of show – much more lively than BMG but not quite up to the frenetic pace of 'Oh Boy'. In addition, it featured most of the performers he had used in the past and voices began to whisper that maybe – just maybe – the golden era was on the downward slope. In 1960 the rumours became fact when the IBA (Independent Broadcasting Authority) made a statement complaining of too much rock 'n' roll on TV. The warning bell that had tinkled up to then became a full throated toll – spelling out the end of an era. It came as no

Meeting a Royal!
(L to R) Maggie, Les Dawson, Laura Lee, H.R.H. Prince Philip and Peters & Lee

surprise, therefore, when a short time later, we heard that we were about to start a grand tour of the UK. Having already suffered the exhausting itinerary of being on the road for months on end, the idea did not appeal to me one bit.

Even within the Vernons Girls themselves, cracks were beginning to appear. Barbara (the Head Girl) had already left to get married and the twins – Ann and Mary – had decided to pursue solo careers. It was with some sadness and a lot of soul searching that I, too, decided to leave the group and form a double act with the stunning redhead by the name of Jean Ryder. The more I thought of it, the better the idea became for Jean – like me – was classically trained and we enjoyed singing the same type of songs. Miss Finegan said at the time "Darlings – now the corner stones are leaving, it is only a matter time before the group will collapse". Shortly afterwards her words proved prophetic and in the early months of 1961, the Vernons Girls – as we knew them – were disbanded. Later, the powers that be decided to revive the group but as a trio – the sexy Maureen Kennedy, Samantha Jones (a comparative newcomer) and Frances Lee and they enjoyed quite a successful career. Meanwhile, Jean and I worked hard rehearsing our new act and we looked forward to a new career as a vocal duo under the new name – THE TWO TONES.

Thankfully, I was able to keep in touch with so many of the girls and, even now after all these years, I am so pleased that we are still in contact today. We were a family, and like all families we shared our emotions – our hopes and our disappointments, our hurts and our moments of joy. We shared, too, the ecstasy of a new romance and the pain at the end of an old one. And when, as previously described, the Vernons Girls finally disbanded, it was the end of an era that would never quite be the same again. The 16 strong group that exploded onto the TV screens in the late Fifties was confined to the history books and filed under the heading "legendary".

In tribute, therefore, will you allow me space in this book to document for posterity, the names and a brief description of the girls who shared the glory, the excitement and the fame of those wonderful days when pop music was clean and innocent and, above all, fun – when the Vernons Girls became part of show business folk-lore and were loved, even revered, by those millions of pop fans who switched on their televisions sets, week after week, to immerse themselves in the music that they, and we, loved so much. I'll simply call this next chapter – "The Girls in the VGs".

CHAPTER 8

The Girls in the V.G.s

Until the invasion from the Wirral, when the five of us crossed the Mersey to join the group, all the girls not only lived in Liverpool but actually worked for Vernons Pools for a living – at least up until the time we began appearing on television and had to spend more and more time in London. Although the group had turned professional before we joined, to my knowledge, the majority – although finding fame *without* fortune – did not harbour any real ambition, or desire, to be in show business and when the group disbanded in 1960, were quite happy to return to Vernons in Liverpool and resume the type of work they had done before.

They were all really nice girls in the true sense of the word and, surprisingly, bearing in mind that 16 young and attractive young ladies could be a hotbed for jealousy and bitchiness, we all got on famously. Obviously sharing four to a room whilst living away from home, meant the forming of special bonds between room mates, but in times of crisis (broken hearts, especially) we became, as previously mentioned, one – a frightening thought for any male miscreant responsible for causing the condition.

Only one girl in the group was married – **Helen Taylor** (from the 'Birkenhead Five'). She was stunning to look at with legs that went on for ever, a superb figure and jet black hair and it was no wonder that the 'powers-that-be' decided to make the exception and invite her to join – despite her obvious handicap!

Attractive **Barbara Mitchell**, Head Girl 'par excellence', with blonde hair, great legs –and short sighted! One of the *very* originals.

Auburn haired **Maureen Kennedy** – the 'oh-so-sexy' one both on and off the screen, who was later to marry Mike Hope of the comedy duo 'Hope & Keen' – and stunning blonde **Lyn Cornel** with the blonde hair and the fabulous 'jazzy' feel to her voice.

Jean Ryder, who I was to team up with to form the 'Two-Tones' was another with great beauty and a superb alto voice but possessed a fiery temper which matched her red hair. The gentle **Peggy Cleary** – so pretty and so well remembered by her Peter Pan collar and a flower at her throat. And so the list goes on – who else was there?

Ann O'Brien – one of the 'twins' and an ex Teddy girl. She was as slim as a reed, with a boyish figure I envy to this day. The other twin was, of course, **Mary Redmond** – so beautiful and so voluptuous with wonderful legs and the highest insteps I've ever seen.

Small and beautiful **Vicky Haseman** with a fabulous voice and a fantastic sense of humour – an ideal 'foil' for her soon-to-be husband, Joe Brown. **Rae Parker** who was so pretty and was, in time, to become a farmers wife and the little 'pocket Venus', **Betty Prescott** (my room mate, along with Vicky) who also had such a great sense of humour. How many's that? Eleven? – a few more to go!! One can't forget **Frances Lea**, the Bridgette Bardot 'look alike'. I think every man who met her fell in love with her – including Billy Fury. **Carmel French,** another of the lovely, gentle, quieter ones and **Dilys Jones** who left the group to become an actress and was regularly seen in bit parts – particularly 'Coronation Street'. Another was **Vera Brooks**, tall slim with a beautiful posture and flawless skin. What sickened me was – she quite often went to bed without removing her make up and she never got a pimple! If I had done that, even once, I'd have a CROP of pimples fermenting the next day. What a lucky girl! Another destined to marry was the lovely **Joyce Baker**. Her prettiness won the heart of one of the rock'n'roll greats – singer Marty Wilde. Finally there was the lovely **Gill Graham** a dancer, and one of twins (sadly she died some time after leaving the group) and **Eleanor Russell**, another dancer – so tiny, so pretty and so nice (still is!). The final two are **Sally Sallis**, acceptable for her lovely looks and instantly recognisable by the prominent gap in her teeth and **Sheila Prytherch**, one of the youngest of the Vernons Girls, who joined the group after working with the world famous Tiller Girls. (She can still kick her height to this day!) Gravel voiced singer Tommy Bruce, whom she later married, was her boyfriend at that time. For those of you counting, you will have realised that the sixteen Vernons Girls have now become twenty. (Modesty prevented me from mentioning myself) but for the period when we reached the height of our fame, there *was* the odd change and those I have written of were the main performers over the period. The Vernons Girls were a phenomenon and I was so proud to have been part of them.

As a foot note to the above, although pointing out that the girls had little interest in continuing their careers in show business, five actually did follow that path and each with success. Ann O'Brien, who later married Mel Simmonds (who courted her at the Colonnade Hotel when we 'gained' our liberation!) returned to show business as one of the 'Pearls' vocal duo – along with Lyn Cornel. Lyn, as a soloist, had had an entry into the pop charts with 'Never on a Sunday' (it stayed in the Hit Parade for a total of 9 weeks reaching a high at No. 20) but after joining up with Ann, entered the charts four more times – the last in 1974 with a song titled G.U.I.L.T.Y. This stayed on the lists for ten weeks and got as high as No. 10. Eventually they decided to split and Lyn joined the world famous James Last Orchestra, travelling all over the world. She later married, inevitably, a musician – drummer Andy White who became famous for his playing on the early Beatles hits. Ann joined the Breakaway vocal group for a short time then, in 1974, became a full-time member of the Ladybirds. The third girl who found vocal success was Sheila Prytherch. Sheila decided on a solo career and, in time, would win the prestigious talent show 'New Faces'. With theatres closing week by week, the only avenue of work regularly open to her was the club circuit and this, she took by storm, becoming a great favourite with the regulars. She toured abroad extensively with equal success and was seldom, if ever, out of work. Today she still sings and, with Penny Lightfoot and I, form the trio – The Vernons Girls who are still in demand. The story behind the reformation, as personally requested by Cliff Richard, is one I will tell in a later chapter.

Ann O'Brien and Lyn Cornel who formed 'The Pearls' vocal duo when the Vernons Girls broke up

CHAPTER 9

The Two Tones

Our first task as the Two Tones was to find an agent and we eventually signed up with Peter Charlesworth the best friend of Benny Hill, who later was to play such an important part in my professional career. We worked so hard learning songs (with each song we had full band parts written) and Jean's mum made us some lovely 'frocks'. We requested Peter to try and find work for us away from the UK in order for us to 'break in' the act, iron out any mistakes and generally find our feet. We attended an audition for Michael Black (the brother of the wonderful songwriter/lyricist Don Black) who was looking for new artistes to tour the American Air Force bases in Germany.

We were offered the job and within days set off for Wiesbaden, which was to be our base for the next few months. It was winter and travelling was difficult, if not impossible. The chosen acts were divided into 'mini shows' with four acts in each show and the unit would then stay together for the length of the contract. We travelled to a different US base each evening in a mini bus and on many an occasion we had to pull over to the side of the road to allow the driver to put chains around the wheels. It was the only way we would have got home! It was petrifying at times and an experience I would not wish to repeat in a hurry. The shows themselves, however, proved of great benefit to us and we learned quickly. It was a wonderful grounding and we learned to cope with bad, rude audiences and accompanists who couldn't read music (we nicknamed one pianist 'elbows' and another 'knuckles' 'cos they sure didn't play using fingers!) One venue we worked didn't even have a piano – but the show must go on, and we survived. We felt so sorry, one evening, for one of the acts touring with us – a lovely man called Syd Wright. Syd was a wonderful xylophonist and coupled with his one line throwaway gags, presented an act which the Americans loved. Poor Syd, after struggling through the snow and ice with the rest of us, arrived at the base and began to unload his belongings. Stage suit, music, hammers

– but something was missing. His xylophone! He'd forgotten to pack the most important part of his act and could only look on as the rest of us added extra songs etc. to our programmes to make up the time.

The venues (or bases) on which we worked were very contrasting. In the E.M. Messes (enlistment men), they did not want to know unless (a) they could see through your dress or better still (b) you were prepared to take it off. If neither was on offer, they simply amused themselves by playing the slot machines and ignored you totally. We were given some wonderful advice by the brilliant trumpet star Kenny Baker who told us "Girls – the secret in working the E.M. bases is to start with a fast tempo upbeat number, put another in the middle and finish the same way. Then get off stage, into your bus and get off home". We took his advice and survived the course! On the other hand the NCOs mess (Non Commissioned Officers) was certainly an improvement but the officers mess was the tops – similar to appearing in a classy night club with excellent musicians and – on the odd occasion – a full size band. The officers were gentlemen and often were accompanied by their wives – always very elegant ladies. It was a joy to be there and our experiences at that end of the scale were ones to remember. Most important of all though was the improvement in the act and by the time we returned to England we were confident enough to face the future.

To our delight, we were informed that we were to go on tour with the Max Bygraves show. In addition to the great man himself, (we became great friends during the run and remain so to this day) the cast included Benson Dulay & Co. (illusionists), The Delrinas (adagio act), The Cycling Kirks, The Lynton Boys, 'Monsewer' Eddie Gray (from 'The Crazy Gang'), a young teenager by the name of Anthony Bygraves and Goldie, The Wonder Horse. It was a lovely show for all the family and we found that our experiences in Germany had paid off – our act was going well., In fact, the only problem we had was avoiding the droppings from Goldie who preceded us!

Part of the off stage crew at that time was a rather elegant young man who went under the title of 'gofor'. His job was to `go for` this and `go for` that and one day, I was waiting for him to vacate the backstage phone box in order that I could ring Mum and Dad and it was not difficult to hear his conversation. He was calling someone 'Sir' constantly and his 'BBC' accent seemed so out of place in a variety theatre. Some time later when we were talking together I said to him "You're not what you seem Colin – you're hiding a secret". He looked a little startled then said "I don't want a soul to know this Maggie so promise me you won't tell. You see, I'm soon to join the Board of the Family Business and it is their idea for me to learn from the bottom up. My father is Chairman of Associated Rediffusion TV and my uncle is Chairman of Wembley Stadium and Southdown Motor Coaches. I've studied at university and am now learning the theatre business from the inside. Please don't say anything will you?" Of course, I agreed for Colin was a lovely boy and popular with everyone. Despite his 'posh' upbringing, however, I would like to place on record that *I* was the one who taught him the joy of eating fish and chips out of a newspaper for which he was eternally grateful.

Some time later Max, who desperately wanted Anthony to continue with his education and *not* follow his footsteps into show business yet a while, was arguing the point with his son when Colin walked past.

"Hey Colin" said Anthony "You've had a good education, haven't you?" Colin agreed. "And what about university?" Anthony continued "You've been there too?"

Again Colin agreed. Anthony turned to his Dad in triumph. "There you are Dad" he said "Colin's had all that education, all that money can buy, and what good has it done him. Look where *he's* ended up". I

Maggie Stredder & Jean Ryder – 'The Two Tones'

50

choked hard trying to keep my promise to Colin not to tell but who knows? Today Colin is probably Chairman of ITV, BBC or BskyB or a dozen other major companies. *That's* where it got him!

The big finale of the show was spectacular, to say the least. Each act in turn was re-introduced to the audience and all wore black with the exception of the gloves which were white. Max, being the star, was the final artiste to take his applause and as the audience clapped, cheered and stamped their feet in approval, we would quickly take our places in a single line stretching from one side of the stage to the other (no – it *wasn't* tallest on the right, shortest on the left!) At a given point, the lights would black out except for the ultra-violet lamps which reflected on the white gloves, giving what is known as a 'black light effect'. It appeared to the audience that the glowing hands were suspended in the air with a life of their own. The music switched into Max's big hit 'You Need Hands' and we all moved our hands in a choreographed routine. It was wonderfully effective and nearly always brought the house down! That is, until my partner Jean decided to put her foot in it – or should I say hand! I began to notice that her time keeping was beginning to get worse and worse and there were times where she barely made the stage following the introduction of our act. On this particular show, she made the stage safely enough but was nowhere to be seen when the music struck up the finale 'walk down'. Each act was acknowledged by an off stage voice and when it announced 'The Two Tones', I took the bow all on my own – a veritable 'One Tone'! On came Max to tumultuous applause, the lights blacked out and the orchestra struck up 'You Need Hands'. The hands went into their disciplined routine and Jean arrived side stage in a panic realising that she was, once again, late and in trouble. Now if she had slipped on to the end of the line it might not have been so bad and many of the audience might not have noticed but our position was either side of Max – slap bang in the middle of the stage and Jean decided to go for broke. The sight that sent the audience into hysterics was a stage full of glowing hands, all following the same movements in regimental style and a rogue pair of hands that suddenly appeared from the wings, completely disorientated, weaving their way from stage left to stage centre before finally finding their place and joining in with the others. The audience probably thinking it was part of the show roared their appreciations and the curtain fell. Max exploded and left poor Jean in no doubt what would happen if she ever did that again. I just looked for a hole to climb into!

There was one other time that Jean fell out with Max but I guess she could not be fully held responsible. The great love of his life (apart from his darling wife Blossom) was his Rolls Royce and he handled it like royalty. Inside and out, it gleamed and every speck of dust had to be meticulously removed before it could be driven. It was the apple of Max's eye and he treated it like a living member of his family. We were highly honoured, therefore, to be offered a lift back to our hotel at the end of the show one evening. We climbed into the back seat and revelled in the luxury we were afforded, waving to passers by with the dignified and gentle hand movement reserved for those blessed with a high station in life. The engine was so quiet it was barely audible and the vehicle, so beautifully balanced on its deluxe springs, gently rocked as it traversed the far-from-even road. It was such a wonderful sensation – at first! It was Jean who began to change colour fist. Her normal complexion paled before settling for a delicate shade of green and her eyes showed the first signs of panic as she realised that Vesuvius was about to erupt. I was not far behind but Jean won the competition to alter the delicate colours that decorated the car's interior and once again, Max was not best pleased. He said little but we were never offered a lift again in his beautiful limousine. I can't think why?

When the tour finally came to an end, we were pleased to learn from Peter (Charlesworth) that we were to embark on another variety show set to travel. I say 'pleased' because it meant a constant wage coming in but it was difficult to accept the fact that one of the reasons we had decided to break from the Vernons Girls was because of the offer to tour and yet, here we were – as the Two Tones – virtually living on the road. Life has a funny way of teaching you a lesson. Nevertheless, off we went on the shuttle-stop merry-go-round of one night stands in a show headlined by Robert Horton – the singer/actor from TVs Western hit show 'Wagon Train'. Co-starring with Robert were my dear friends – Cliff Richard & The Shadows, plus the Trebletones and the Dallas Boys. It was a happy show and we shared lot of laughs especially with the latter for they possessed a very wicked sense of humour and kept both Jean and I on the continual look-out for practical jokes! As far as the boys were concerned *every* day was April Fools Day!

I never tire of repeating the great pleasure I get in watching an embryo talent emerge and in time, climb to the pinnacle of success – and stardom! Such was the case of three lovely Irish lads who joined us on yet another tour, headlined by Nina & Frederick with ourselves, Saveen & Daisy Mae and our friends from over the Irish Sea –The Harmonichords. Their act was similar to the better known Morton Fraser Harmonica Gang and equally as good but the main problem they had was simply that of material – they could only do twelve minutes.

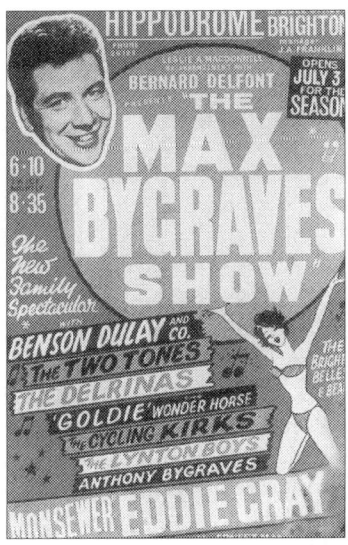

Seeing double –
Max and Anthony Bygraves

'The Two Tones' appearing on the
'Max Bygraves Show'

"I wanna tell you a story" – backstage with Max and husband Jim

John Stokes, Dec & Con Cluskey –
The Bachelors

Between two showbiz legends
– Bing Crosby and Fred Astaire

The lovely Des O'Connor

*The 'Ladybirds' with
Des O'Connor & David Frost*

*Reording a TV show with Dusty
Springfield
– but just out of shot (honest!)*

*Teaching the 'Hand Jive' on
'The Michael Barrymore Show'*

*The Ladybirds x 2
(note the matching glasses)*

*The Ladybirds x 3 – Maggie,
Marion Davies and Gloria George*

*A very happy Mum
with newborn
daughter Anna
(& Marion Davies)*

A young and handsome Benny Hill

*Benny with his friend
(and our agent) Peter Charlesworth.
1956*

*Gloria & I share the
Ladybirds with some
'fat bird' who wouldn't
go away*

*The Benny Hill 'Gang' (L to R) Ted Taylor (musical assoc.), me, Ronnie Aldrich,
Jon Jon Keefe, Benny, Ann, actress Kathy Staff, Laura, Jackie Wright,
Henry McGee and falling over at the front, producer/director Dennis Kirkland*

It was a happy show and all the acts blended well with each other but strangely, the top-of-the-bill, whilst friendly with the cast, could not, it seemed, transfer that warmth into their personal lives and were often heard quarrelling loudly. Nina was the most stunningly beautiful lady, whom we christened the' Ice Maiden' and Frederick was as near to perfection as any male could be, and together, on stage, they produced magic. Off stage, however, the harmony struggled.

The Irish trio struggled, too, but their problem was one of cash and they found it difficult to make ends meet. It seemed natural, therefore, when we were appearing for the week at the Liverpool Empire, that I invite them to meet my Mum and Dad in Birkenhead to enjoy some home cooked delicacy – egg and chips – made to order.

The boys continued their career and one evening in Manchester, in an attempt to lengthen the rather short presentation, they added some vocals to their harmonica playing and the rest is history. They changed their name to The Bachelors and they never looked back.

Only a few weeks ago, whilst compiling this book, I worked again with John Stokes, the founder and original member of the group, at the Grand Theatre Wolverhampton. He was there working with his new trio – the Bachelors with John Stokes – and he reminded me of the story.

"Maggie" he said "You will never realise what those meals meant to us. Without your help – and, of course, your Mum's superb chips- we would never have survived!" It's a pleasure John and if you're ever passing our humble abode in the near future – the chip pan's at the ready!

The end of the Two Tones was in sight, however, when Jean's love affair with songwriter Mike Hawker deepened and they decided to marry. At first it did not seem to affect our working relationship and we were still available for whatever work came our way but when Mike started to write for Helen Shapiro and the hits began to flow, Jean decided that she had had enough and the time was right for her to quit. I had no quarrel with her decision and did not blame her in any way. In her position, I would probably have done the same thing but, nevertheless, I was now on my own, up a gum tree with no work coming in – and I was very, very broke!

CHAPTER 10

Stoney broke but Lionel Blair saves the day

I moved into digs with a lovely lady called Kitty Laurenson. Although she was not connected to show business in any way, we had much in common and most of it was due to us both being broke! In addition she had two young children to clothe and feed and between us, we shared a very miserable existence. To make matters worse, it was now winter time and very, very cold. We could not afford to heat the flat and could hardly scrape up enough money to buy food, with the result I became desperately thin and extremely bronchitic! It was the lowest point of my life and yet, through all the trauma and the desperation, I never once thought of returning home to my Mum and Dad in Birkenhead. Maybe it was pride – or perhaps optimism that something would turn up. Whatever it was, I kept going but the period dragged on and on and appeared to have no end until one day – out of the blue – the phone rang!

It was agent Peter Charlesworth who, as well as looking after the Two Tones (as was) also managed dancer/singer Lionel Blair, amongst many others.

"Maggie" he said "I've something you might be interested in"! What an understatement I thought, but waited for him to continue.

"Lionel (Blair) is doing a months cabaret at the Colony Club in London. He already has two dancers but wants two girl singers who can 'move' and we've asked Angela from the TV game show 'Beat The Clock' to be one, will you be the other? They'll pay you £40.00 a week!" I nearly dropped the phone in shock, joy and relief. God it was a fortune. Yes! Yes! Yes! And with Lionel Blair too, whom I'd already worked with on the TV show 'New Look'. The sun began to shine again and I climbed from my valley of despair but if I felt that my luck had now changed – time was to prove just how fortuitous that phone call was to be. I was on the way back.

The show opened and it was a joy to be working again. The business was good and Lionel's act was, not surprisingly, very polished and very well received. Being in London, it was convenient for many star names to drop in but the face I recognised most was that of Benny Hill – probably because he was there most nights. As I have said before, he was a close friend of Peter Charlesworth and the two sat side by side giving us their support, like the good mates they were.

I had first met Benny in 1957 through Peter (I was a very skinny and very new Vernons Girl) and he had boasted to the comedian of his good fortune in discovering this 'nest of crumpet' living just down the road from Benny's mansion flat in the Edgeware Road. The 'nest' referred to was, of course, the Colonnade Hotel and the 'crumpet' was the delectable Vernons Girls. It was a mere stones throw away and unable to believe his good luck, invited the agent to prove it. "Invite them to a party at my place" he said and Peter did just that!

Bearing in mind it was early days and we had not yet won our freedom, he cunningly invited Miss Finegan to meet Benny and having gained her approval (and with her permission) a few of us went to the get-together. Two memories stand out of that first meeting. The first was being offered a sausage roll by the comic. I refused.

"Don't tell me you're dieting?" he said, but I still demurred.

"Bloody Hell!" he retorted "I've seen more fat on a chip!" I laughed for it was the first time I had heard that expression. The second memory, however, was more intimate for if I had any notion that Benny Hill fancied me – I was to think again for he made it obvious he fancied Vicki. Nevertheless, we formed a friendship that was to last over 30 years and indeed, much of my showbiz life was spent working with him. He really was a very special mate! It was no surprise therefore, on the opening night of my cabaret debut with Lionel, to receive a special 'good luck' present from him. Not the flowers I hoped for and expected. No – not from Benny Hill! What he sent with his love and blessing, was a sausage roll complete with a plate of chips. We laughed about that for years afterwards. And talking of food, my first week's wage was spent stocking up Kitty's fridge freezer and larder, as well as paying some bills and turning on the heat again. Once again we were warm and well fed.

Towards the end of the engagement, Lionel was asked to make a record and that simple request, along with Lionel's agreement to actually make the recording and to choose the two songs to be recorded, became another milestone in my life. The 'A' side was predetermined but for the

'B' side, Lionel selected one of the songs from his cabaret act – a song in which I featured, singing a very high coloratura obligato , and of course, he wanted me to join him on the recording. With great trepidation, I joined him at the studios and, for the first time, saw what I can only describe as 'real' session singers – The Nigel Brook Singers to be exact – and they were quite superb! They too, were there to lend their harmonious voices to the Lionel Blair record and after it was all over, to my astonishment and delight, Nigel approached me, impressed with what I had done and invited me to do some sessions with him. Now – to be a session singer you have to read music as quickly as reading a book or newspaper and unknowingly to me at the time, the years I spent studying piano and taking singing lessons suddenly became of great value and meant I could join the prestigious Nigel Brook Singers without fear of embarrassment. I was on cloud nine. In the space of four weeks my life had taken another dramatic turn and I was now back in the business and back in the big time!

Amongst the girls in the group was a beautiful dark haired girl called Gloria George. Her father was Persian and her mother was an English Rose and the combination of European and Middle Eastern looks had produced a real beauty. Whilst in the recording studios and performing my part of the highly pitched vocal backing, she had (I found out later) been looking at me and thinking – Now that's a *real* session singer! Co-incidentally , I had had exactly the same thought as she performed her part of the vocal proceedings and it was inevitable that we should become friends. She was quite new to the type of life she was now leading for she had been a singer/dancer in mainly West End shows. For a long time she had been dating a gorgeous looking Scotsman from Edinburgh and becoming weary and a little frustrated at his reluctance to make the union more permanent, she finally took the bull by the horns and actually proposed to him. He turned her down with the lame reason that marriage was not for him as he wished to concentrate solely on his career. "One day" he said "I want to become a star". He was proved right and he did. His name was Sean Connery!

Nigel Brook was as good as his word and we appeared on the TV series 'Stars and Garters'. Alan Braden was the musical director of that particular production and later, with the Ladybirds, I was to work with Alan on all of his TV shows. One of the regulars who appeared on the show along with resident compere Ray Martine and lovely vocalist Kathy Kirby, was a gravel voice singer called Tommy Bruce who had a number of hit songs – the most recognised was 'Ain't Misbehavin' which entered the charts in May 1960 and stayed in the top twenty for sixteen weeks. It never made the top spot but did get as high as N. 3. Tommy was another rock'n'roller who fell for the charms of a Vernons Girl and married Sheila Prytherch. Sadly the marriage did not survive the course but Sheila later remarried, this time to a member of the police force – Clive Parker – and they have since enjoyed a long and happy union together. Our friendship has also lasted throughout the years and, as previously mentioned, Sheila still works with me today (along with Penny Lightfoot) as a three handed 'Vernons Girls' act – still singing for our supper and still touring, particularly with The Solid Gold Rock'n'Roll Show along with Marty Wilde & The Wildcats, Joe Brown & The Bruvvers, Eden Kane and John Leyton – but more of that later!

By now Glo and I had become close friends and, once again, the thoughts of re-forming the duo entered my head. I approached her with the idea and to my delight she agreed immediately. We decided at the same time that, although predominantly working as a double act, we would continue to be available as session singers – probably as an insurance, in view of my past experiences. The final piece of the jig-saw was to find ourselves a name, for we both felt that the Two Tones was not suitable. We turned suggestion after suggestion over and out of our minds before we finally agreed that the one name which fitted us well and we both loved was the name that was to become recognised throughout the world as one of the best female singing groups to come from Gt. Britain. Even today it is spoken of in awe, by those who still remember. The legendary 'Ladybirds' had been born!

CHAPTER 11

The Ladybirds back the stars – including Bing Crosby

Gloria and I began working as a duo and were thrilled to be given a contract to appear in the weekly BBC/TV 'Val Doonican Show' – his first as a solo performer. We were required to do our own 'spot' in addition to vocally backing Val (in vision) and it was a wonderfully warm feeling to know I had not been forgotten by the viewers. Once again the 'fan' letters started to pour in and it was a great feeling to know that the 'Girl with the Glasses' was back on the box! As a gimmick, however, (you see – Jack Good wasn't the only one with good ideas!) we decided that, whilst working as a duo, Gloria should be wearing matching glasses to mine – and so she did. We stayed that way until we added the third girl to the act then reverted back, once again, to me being the only one with the specs!

In addition to the lovely letters we received, offers of work also started to arrive – mainly as backing singers both on TV and records and I began to realise that, although our voices blended well together and made such a good sound, a third voice was becoming essential to create fuller harmonies so necessary in the type of work we were now doing. With that in mind, therefore, I enlisted another girl called Barbara Moore and the 'Ladybirds' became a trio.

We went from strength to strength but our very first big moment came in 1964 when we received a call booking us for a recording session at the Pye Studios in London. The booker, or fixer as they are sometimes called, would ring me up with simple requests and instructions. They would sound something like this –

"Hi Maggie – can you do the Ladybirds, 2 to 5, 7 to 10 p.m. Pye Studios – 3rd October?" or similar, specifying 3 boys and 3 girls with similar directions, and we would turn up at the given time, not knowing who we were to record with and only the name of the musical director as the contact.

On this occasion the M.D. was Ken Woodman and when we arrived we found the singer we were to back was someone we had never heard of before but she struck us as rather odd for she stood waiting to perform in her bare feet. Yes – it was Sandie Shaw and the song we recorded that day was 'There's Always Something There To Remind Me'.

It entered the charts on 8th October 1964 and became a No. 1 hit. It stayed in the Top Twenty for a total of 11 weeks and Sandie Shaw was to become the only girl soloist at that time to have three No. 1's, ('There's Always Something There' plus 'Long Live Love' in May '65 and 'Puppet On A String' twenty two months later) and the Ladybirds recorded with her on all three. My inexperience, however, in the method of recording at that time nearly lost me my voice for in the chorus of 'There's Always Something There To Remind Me' you will hear a very high voice singing top 'A's behind the title line of the song. The recording engineer repeatedly asked Sandie and the various sections of the orchestra to repeat the phrase again and again and again in order to get the correct sound balance and like good pros we belted out the harmony with me rising to the high notes again and again and again. Finally, after almost forty attempts, the engineer finally was satisfied and he

'The Ladybirds' provide the backing on three No. 1 hits for Sandie Shaw

announced "Right – happy with that! Now lets add the Ladybirds vocal backing!" and to my horror I realised that, each time Sandie sung the chorus and we had dutifully joined in, our microphone had been turned off and our musical presence had been not required until instructed. The result was a very hoarse Ladybird trying to again reach the high notes with a voice that was slowly disappearing into a stage whisper. The next time you hear the record, listen carefully and sympathise.

It is a well known piece of musical history that Sandie was entered into the Eurovision Song Contest in 1967 with 'Puppet on a String' with us – The Ladybirds – as her 'on stage' vocal backing. The BBC flew us to Vienna for the contest and it was one of the most exciting evenings of my life but to have won put the icing on the cake. We were besieged by the press both after the show itself and again the next morning but eventually we found our way to the airport and dutifully queued at the check-in desk prior to joining the aircraft for the flight home. During her career, Sandie Shaw was managed by a strong, dominant lady by the name of Eve Taylor and, as we patiently waited to register, Eve and Sandie appeared. Seeing the queue, Eve decided that such a common practice was not in keeping for her protégé – some one who, the evening before, had *only* won the 'Eurovision Song Contest'! She marched poor Sandie, looking desperately embarrassed, to the head of the line and put her tickets and passports on the counter. The check-in steward smiled and said "I am sorry Madam, but you will have to go to the back of the queue!" Eve pulled herself to her full height and glared at the man.

"Young man" she shouted "we have no intention of queueing. Don't you know who this is?" She pointed at Sandie and we (and she) cowered in embarrassment.

"Well" said the steward, keeping his cool and his dignity, "She's not the Queen of England". Eve Taylor glared at him for just a moment. "After last night" she yelled "she *is* the bloody Queen of England!!" The recollection of their conversation is not wholly accurate for Eve's language was of a more colourful nature and suffice it to say that the word bloody was not the one she selected – it was rather more Anglo – Saxon and more commonly heard on a building site. Regardless, however, her bombastic attitude and command of the less acceptable words in the English Language failed to impress the Austrian airline employee and poor Sandie with her blaspheming manager in tow, retired to the rear of the queue as mere mortals.

The success we had with Sandie prompted the flood gates to open and offers to record with all the big stars of the day poured in. I can recall turning up to a recording one day with the voice of Wales – Tom Jones. The full vocal backing consisted of the three Ladybirds plus one more girl and four male singers and soon we were hard at work in putting 'Daughter of Darkness' on disc. Finally, the sound engineers had done their balancing, the orchestra had ironed out the arrangement, Tom was ready and we awaited the OK from control. "OK" came the voice "we're ready to go – the red light's on – lets go for a take". The orchestra was in full flow and as I stood up to sing my solo obligato, the studio was deafened by a rasping sound similar to an elephant suffering from severe flatulence. The entire company collapsed in hysterics – including Tom, who had a wild sense of humour. We looked around for the culprit and he was easy to spot for he was hugging the cause of the noise – a large 'whoopee cushion' to his chest and loving every second of the chaos he had caused. He was one of the male backing singers by the name of Reg Dwight – a freelance session singer who later went solo and changed his name, but never lost his love of practical jokes. You're a naughty boy, Elton John, but we all love you just the same!

Recording was long and hard but always varied. We never knew what to expect when we turned up for work at the studios and on many occasions, it was not what we expected. A good example was one day, whilst anticipating the normal distribution of vocal arrangements which, as previously mentioned, we were expected to read, then sing on sight, we were somewhat surprised, therefore, to be addressed by the artiste we were supposed to back that day – American singer/songwriter, Rod McKuen. He informed us that he had booked the studio to record an opera he had written and we had been brought in to play the parts. He handed the music to me and, totally dumbfounded at what we were expected to do, I distributed the various character roles to those I felt best suited. To Annie, I gave the part of the wicked witch and being the Boss – I gave myself the role of the beautiful damsel. We completed the recording over four days – three sessions a day – and, when completed, Rod was delighted. For us, however, it was an experience – the first and, I hope, the last! We *did* enjoy it but it was really not us and I would rather not attempt anything of this nature again. Us – opera singers? I think not!

One lovely story, regarding another American star, was the day we arrived at the studios to discover we were to provide the vocal backing for two legendary performers who were combining their talents to produce an album – Bing Crosby and Fred Astaire. As thrilled as I was to meet and work with these showbiz greats, Joan Baxter, one of the other session singers booked for the recording, was ecstatic. "I must ring my Mum during the break for lunch" she said "and tell her who we are working with. She is a Bing Crosby fanatic and she'll just die". As soon as the mid-day break was called, Joan dashed to the phone and was just about to tell her Mum the news, when who should walk by, at just that moment, but the man himself. Without as much as a 'by your leave' – Joan thrust the phone into his hand and said "Bing – say hallo to my Mum – her name is Harriet". Bing, without turning a hair, and in that very recognisable voice of his, spoke into the mouthpiece. "Hi, Harriet – this is Bing Crosby. Howya doin'". For all the effect it had on Joan's mum, it could have been the local butcher. In her broad Yorkshire accent she replied "Ee – is that you Bing? Me arthritis is killing me!"

"Well honey" replied the crooner "don't you worry. You just sit yourself down with a large brandy – no, make that **two** large brandies – and you'll feel much better." Joan's mum, the Bing fanatic who we felt would just die at the thought of speaking to her hero, refused even now to show her excitement or, worse still, to admit her personal worship of the man.

"Our Joan's Dad" she said "thought you were wonderful!!" Bing was unable to say another word for Harriet's phlegmatic reply struck a funny bone and he left us to enjoy his lunch, still roaring with laughter at the conversation.

CHAPTER 12

Fun & Laughter with the 'Des O'Connor Show'

Amongst the many other wonderful shows we worked on – probably the one which gave us the most pleasure was the 'Des O'Connor Show'. Not only was he great fun to be with, but so too, were many of his weekly guests. There are no prizes in guessing the maddest, craziest and daftest one of them all – it had to be Freddie Starr! When being interviewed by Des, he was unpredictable enough but when the other guests took their turn on camera, Freddie became uncontrollable.

One moment of chaos came when Freddie was booked to appear along with Elaine Paige. Freddie had finished his chat with Des and moved off camera as Des introduced Elaine. Now, Elaine was adamant that if you booked her – you booked her dog, a white Terrier by the name of 'Tugger'. As the music played her on to the set, she joined Des on the settee and 'Tugger' settled down beside her – unfazed by the lights, the music and the applause. That was, until Freddie stepped in! He appeared out of shot, trailing a stuffed dog behind him on a lead. 'Tugger' went berserk, leaping off the couch and in a frenzy of attempted sexual fulfilment, tried to have his wicked way with the stuffed animal. Realising that his ardour was not being reciprocated and his declaration of love was in one direction only, he succumbed from being one with arduous intentions to one with vengeful desire – and proceeded to tear the poor inanimate object limb from limb. If the furry toy was reduced to shreds, it also knocked the stuffing out of Des and he disappeared backwards in a spray of hysterical tears of laughter, whilst the ever elegant Elaine summoned up all her dignity in trying to separate the two warring beasts and prevent further embarrassment. The audience howled, the cameramen collapsed and we fell about. That show became No. 1 in the ratings for all the wrong reasons!

Freddie was unstoppable. On another show, when all was safely recorded, we retired to the Green Room (the hospitality suite) for drinks and a few snacks. The Producer/Director was Brian Penders, brilliant at

Holding Freddie Starr firmly in his seat

his job and probably, at that time, one of the best in the business. Unfortunately, Brian had suffered a serious accident to his leg but bravely directed the show with the help of crutches. It was arranged that Brian would go into hospital the following morning for an operation that, he hoped, would help repair the damage. Now, as the name suggests, Thames Television is adjacent to the River Thames and, being summer, all the windows were open. This was too much for Freddie! Full of initial compassion, he approached Brian and asked how the accident happened. Brian told him and Freddie remarked that Brian should be in hospital. Brian took the bait – hook, line and sinker!

"There's no problem" he said "I'm due to go in first thing in the morning" . "Ah" said Fred, his eyes lighting up with wicked malice "You won't be needing these, then". He took hold of the crutches and lobbed them through the open window and into the Thames. Brian Penders has asked me to say that if any deep sea trawler men fishing in the North Sea, come across a pair of soggy crutches in their fishing nets – please, can he have them back!

There's an old saying that you never repeat the same gag twice but Freddie did – and got away with it, just! The unlucky victim this time was singer Englebert Humperdinck and during the show, E.H. had been posing, showing off to all and sundry, his new and highly expensive diamond-studded Rolex watch. This was too much for the funny man. Once again in the Green Room, he approached the singer and asked to see the timepiece. E.H. was delighted to show it and handed it to Freddie.

"It's brilliant" said Fred "Fantastic!" He looked at it, this time more closely. "Hang on!" he said, and held it up to his ear "It's going slow. I think it's stopped! It's a piece of crap!" and so saying, the watch, worth over four figures, followed the same path as the crutches and with a faint 'plop' disappeared into the depths of the River Thames. "Doesn't time fly!" he said, and we didn't know whether to laugh or cry!

Other guests, too, are worth a mention. June Alyson, the lovely American film star with lots to tell, told of nothing. She only wanted to talk about her grand children and, as hard as Des tried, would discuss nothing else! Cyd Charise was the most beautiful of ladies and my abiding memory of her was passing her dressing room door and seeing her 'warming up'. She stood facing the wall, her body touching the paintwork and her right leg stretching to the ceiling. Both hands held the right ankle tightly and such was the length of her incredible legs, it looked an almost impossible position, yet she made it with ease, even though, at that time, she must have been well into her late fifties. What dedication!

Another guest who caused panic for reasons different to Freddie, was Oliver Reed. Ollie was immensely popular with the stage crew, floor staff, musicians and us. He was simply a lovely guy but he liked (nay – loved!) a drink. It did not take him long to reach happy land and he would blunder about the studio finding everything so much fun. He would knock over music stands and whilst the musicians scrabbled on the floor desperately looking for their charts, Ollie would giggle like a naughty schoolboy. Once, when being interviewed by Des, he decided to tell the world that he had had his name tattooed on a certain part of his anatomy that was safety stored in his 'Y' fronts. If that was bad enough for Des to cope with, worse was to follow for he then attempted to show the millions watching, proof. How Des managed to prevent the moment that would have shut the programme down for good – only he knows!

I am sure, too, that many will remember the occasion when the very funny comedian Stan Boardman over stepped the mark with his story of the Focke-Wolfe German planes. If you didn't see the show, it doesn't matter for it takes little imagination to guess what came next. His final line "The Fockes bombed our chip shop!" may have brought the house down in the studio but it nearly brought the curtain down on Stan's career, for the TV bosses were too scared to book him in the future and his work, at least for a while, suffered – although I believe his club work doubled and the story they all demand to hear is the one where a special make of German plane flattened his chippie!

One who almost didn't make the show was Whitney Houston. She was fine during rehearsals and for the actual show itself, was to wear the most magnificent evening gown. She was in her dressing room, made up, costumed and ready to step, out when the running order for the show was given to her. She, of course, was down to close the show but when she read that, she and her husband went berserk. It seemed that, in America when you appear on a similar type of show, the top-of-the-bill always goes on first! Brian Penders tried to explain but she was having none of it. Off came the costume and the make up and on went her ordinary day wear. With the show about to commence, Brian and Des finally gave in and she opened – wearing the clothes she had arrived in and with not an ounce of make up. She still stood them in the aisles – what a talent!

There was one name that was continually mentioned to Des and Brian for inclusion in the show but, as he was virtually unknown, they were wary. They both felt that to feature a comic, untried and untested, on the programme might prove difficult for, if he lacked the prime ingredient for successful comedy – timing – or worse still, his material was suspect – it could turn out a disaster. So they deferred. One producer, however, that *was* prepared to give the comedian a break was Dave Clark in the show called 'London Night Out' hosted by Tom O'Connor. Dave had already sampled his zany humour, for he had used him as an audience warm-up man prior to the recording of a Christmas edition of the panel game 'Give Us A Clue'. Such was the impact on the audience, Dave mentally filed his name for the future – and now his time had come. The show was well under way and ventriloquist Ken Wood was performing well with his horse-doll getting big laughs. Our hero was to follow and was standing by, ready to make his TV debut, when a bomb scare was relayed to the studio with the instruction to evacuate. Being the true professional that he was, Dave waited until the vent had finished his routine before asking the audience to leave (Ken was fine but the horse was furious!) By the time the building had been searched and declared safe, there was no studio time available to continue the show and it was shelved. A further date was set and, on that occasion, everything went well. The unknown comic took the studio audience and the TV viewers by storm, especially with his 'cod' ballet routine in which he invited an unsuspecting member

We 'jump the broomstick' with American singing star – Brenda Lee

of the audience to join him in a chaotic rendition of 'Swan Lake' and the next day the funny man's name – Michael Barrymore – was on everybody's lips. Des & Brian have, of course, used him many times since with high success – but on that special evening – a star was born!

Finally, back to the Des O'Connor Show and if we had great success with our contribution to the musical side of the show, we had equal success in another. Des always insisted that when we were not doing what we were contracted to do – singing – we were given seats in the audience very close to him so that he could rely on us to laugh in all the right places. The three of us – Ann Simmonds, Laura Lee and I, all possess what Des considered to be 'hearty chuckles' and it was a great comfort for him to know that we were there when he needed us most.

Sadly for us – and the show – budget cuts began to rear their ugly heads and in 1990, we learned that, as a means of cutting the cost of production, three major changes were being made. The first was to cut down the size of the orchestra, second was to prune the number of scriptwriters and third, sadly for us, was to dispense with the backing singers. All good things must come to an end some time but it was a sad day nevertheless. For all the wonderful times we enjoyed and for all the laughs we had – our thanks to Brian and particularly our old 'mate' Des O'Connor.

CHAPTER 13

'Top Of The Pops'

Probably the most prestigious show ever undertaken by the 'Ladybirds' was 'Top of the Pops' for two main reasons. The first was that we appeared as backing singers on the programme for an incredible 19 years – surely a record that will never, ever be broken. The second, more obvious, in that we appeared with every Band, Group or Artistes who ever made the Top Twenty Charts from 1964 onwards – American and British – and you only have to consider the superstars during that period to realise the company we kept. Because of that particular show and, of course, 'The Benny Hill Show' in which we were involved for 22 years, we became an institution. Trying to recall the great moments from T.O.T.Ps is nigh impossible. We turned up at the studios every week for the entire run, were given our musical directions, recorded the show and went home. It was a blur. Of course, we met all the major stars of the era but even they, too, dissolve into memory and to pick out the stories, the laughs and the dramatic times is too difficult to attempt.

To give you a flavour of the concept, however, I *can* recall the very first showing of 'Top of The Pops' and let me tell you who it featured. The historic date was New Years Day 1964 and the show was transmitted live at 6.36 p.m. from a converted church in Manchester. This show was hosted by Jimmy Saville with the three other chosen disc jockeys – Alan Freeman, David Jacobs and Pete Murray – sharing the rest of the month's shows, i.e. one show each per week. Performing live on that first showing were:–

The Rolling Stones with their second hit 'I Wanna Be Your Man'. This particular song peaked at No. 12 although it stayed in the charts for 16 weeks.

Dusty Springfield with 'I Only Wanna Be With You'. Although this number is still hugely popular to this day, it never reached No 1. It's highest position was No. 4 and it stayed around for 18 weeks.

The Dave Clark five No. 1 in the Charts with 'Glad All Over'

The Hollies with their hit 'Stay'. Not a No. 1 – it only reached No. 8

The Swinging Blue Jeans with 'The Hippy Hippy Shake'. It almost made it to the top spot but not quite and it remained at No. 2. The original lads in the group are still together bar one and working today.

Appearing on film in addition to the above were:–

Cliff Richard and The Shadows with their No. 2 hit 'Don't Talk To Him' (13 weeks in the Top Twenty).

Freddie & The Dreamers – 'You Were Made For Me' which got to No. 3

Gene Pitney – 'Twenty Four Hours From Tulsa'. It got to No. 5. Interesting to note that he never reached No. 1 in the British Charts until he recorded 'Something's Gotten Hold Of My Heart' in January 1989.

The Beatles with 'I Wanna Hold Your Hand'. Where else could it be, but No. 1 – the second of three number ones in a row. ('She Loves You' in August '63 and later 'Can't Buy Me Love' in March '64.) Altogether they had a total of 17 No. 1's (singles) Wow!!

So that was the line up and what a cast!

Our problem was, of course, travelling to Manchester each week from London and, in those days, the train was the only sensible option. The journey took five and a quarter hours and cost £2. 10/- (in old money) single. If you required a sleeper, you added a further £1. 6/- . If you were a 'star' however, you flew at a cost of £9.14/- one way. Guess which mode of transport we chose? (stagecoaches were, of course, no longer in fashion!) The show stayed in Manchester for a further two years before being transferred to London.

What a joy this show was for us. Almost every week, we witnessed the birth of a new star and it was such an experience to watch their careers take off. The show, as I said, was live and it remained so for a long time afterwards. A full orchestra, featuring the very best musicians in the country was provided under the leadership of Johnny Pearson and interestingly, he too, entered the hit parade with his orchestra with the recording of 'Sleepy Shores'. He played the piano solo and watched it climb to No. 8 in the charts – staying in the Top Twenty for 15 weeks. Brilliant!

Having such an orchestra to provide the backing, however, was not to everyone's liking. Tammy Wynette was due to appear on the show singing her hit song 'Stand By Your Man' but at rehearsals, her husband went berserk. Listening to the beautiful arrangement written for this fine orchestra he rushed into Tammy's dressing room yelling "Honey – you're not going on! The band can't read music!" They were, of course brilliant readers but Mr. Wynette wanted, and expected, to hear an exact replica of the backing from the hit record and assumed the orchestra were reading it all wrong. Tammy refused to go on and it took a great deal of diplomacy and a music arranger working all afternoon to re-score the arrangement to the more familiar backing before she consented to appear. I won't add to that scenario nor will I make further comment!

One final story of the Top of The Pops concerns a Party Political Broadcast from the Prime Minister at that time – Edward Heath. Mr. Heath had arrived at the BBC to record his message and found to his concern, that the studio he had been allocated, was next door to TOTPs. It so happens that, on that particular day, the bands appearing were especially loud with the exception of a live appearance from the 'Old Groaner' himself – Bing Crosby and the Director feared a backlash from the politician. On cue, the P.M. entered the studio and in a stern voice demanded to see 'him in charge'. Visualising entombment in the Bloody Tower at least, he approached 'his prominence' in some fear.

"Are you in charge here?" shouted the great man.

"Yessir" trembled the Director "Yes – I am!" The Prime Minister leant towards him and asked

"Any chance of Bing Crosby's autograph?"

That story, I promise, you is true.

Top of The Pops still runs today nearly forty years later and it is still a great thrill to think that we began it all those years ago, on the very day it started.

CHAPTER 14

My Family – the joy of my life

In 1966, I married scriptwriter Roy Tuvey at Bidston Parish Church in Birkenhead. In addition to his writing – he wrote and produced many shows on the old Radio Luxembourg – he was the joint owner of a 'young peoples' club called Tiles, which operated in Oxford Street, London. In time, it became the largest of its type in Europe but sadly, because of new legislation, it had to close its doors. Roy continued to write, however, and enjoyed much success, especially in the TV media.

We had first met eight years before, during our 'freedom' period and I fall madly in love. Sadly however, he was not prepared to accept any long term commitment and we eventually decided to part but in early 1966, to my delight, we met up again and this time there was no holding back. On the 1st October, we tied the knot and I became Mrs. Maggie Tuvey. I had always longed for a family and to our joy, I gave birth to a daughter, Anna, on 23rd November 1968. I had her 'by appointment' for, although wanting a family so very much, I was a devout coward and requested an epidural! The day before, I had done 'Top of the Pops' and, on returning home and knowing that Roy was waiting to transport me to the hospital, I was determined to finish the curtain I was making for the nursery. It was only when I had completed the final stitch that I allowed Roy to start the car. I crawled into bed that night but found it difficult to sleep, anxiously anticipating what was to happen the following day but nevertheless excited at the thought of welcoming my new baby into the world.

It was a long delivery period, much longer than I had expected but, because of the epidural, I felt nothing. I had become so relaxed by now, Roy and I played Scrabble to pass the time! At long last, Anna made her entry and to my great concern, was jaundiced on arrival. If that was not enough, although unaware at the time, it masked a far more serious condition and I was not told until days later that she was suffering from a kidney infection. Not knowing this, however, I took a phone call from a producer at Thames Television, asking if I could do an insert for the 'Max Bygraves Show' the following evening. We had actually recorded the vocals in sound only but now they decided that they wanted us 'in vision'. Could I make it? I thought long and hard and finally told him I probably could, but would let him know a little later. He sounded a bit puzzled and asked me "Where are you? This isn't your home phone number".

"No" I replied "I'm in a maternity hospital!"

There was an audible gasp. "Bloody Hell" said the voice "What are you doing there?" What a stupid question I thought and said "I'll give you three guesses!"

I rang my gynaecologist, asking her permission and she agreed.

"Yes you can do it" she said "As long as you come straight back afterwards!"

I booked the other girls required for the shoot and all was well until we arrived at Thames the following day. I stood on the set and, as directed, posed and mimed to the music. I began to sway and feel faint, the awful feeling of disorientation before blackness descends and you pass out. I prayed hard! "Please God – not now. Please let me get through this!" Well – I did and the producer – William G. Stewart (now the quizmaster in the general knowledge programme '15 to 1') reckoned I was a 'true pro' – a real trouper. The truth of the matter is a lot more simple – I just cannot turn down a job!!

As promised, I returned to the hospital immediately and was increasingly worried at little Anna's condition. She was becoming more ill by the second and two days later, was rushed to the Kings College Hospital in Dulwich by ambulance which saw the need to flash its blue emergency lights and ring its siren. Anna was put into intensive care and I lived in the hospital to be with her. For two weeks we did not know whether she would live or die and, to me, nothing else mattered – it was the worst time of my life. Thank God – she finally pulled through and today, at the age of 32, she is healthy, very beautiful and herself, now, a mother to the light of my life – 7 year old Charlotte Anne Nicholson, a grand daughter I adore!

The trauma surrounding Anna's birth did not sour my ambition to add to my family and 30 months later, I presented Roy with a second child – this time a son we christened Paul. In view of my previous experience,

My lovely daughter Anna with gorgeous grand-daughter Charlotte

when the time came, the hospital was on full alert (the same hospital, the same gynaecologist and the same anaesthetist – nothing like being surrounded by the same friendly faces) but this time all was well. Whereas Anna, despite the jaundiced look, had been an extremely pretty baby, Paul was anything but! His nose was one sided and his ears stuck out, but when he smiled – the sun came out. He beamed with a happiness that lit up his little face and transformed it into one of beauty. He is now 6′ 3″ tall and extremely handsome.

A neighbour, who had actually watched my husband Roy grow up, became their nanny. Mabs has been a second grandmother to them and a surrogate mother to me (my parents were still living in the North) and without her, I could never have continued with my career. She died at the age of 90 and I am given great comfort by the fact that my little Charlotte shares the same birthday. I pray that she has inherited Mabs' strength of character, her sense of humour and above all, her selflessness. She devoted her life to helping others – the greatest gift one can give to anyone.

My handsome son Paul with a 'growing up' Charlotte

CHAPTER 15

A great 'mate' – Benny Hill

Benny Hill was the nicest, kindest and most gentle man I have ever met. I know of no-one who can remember him saying an unkind word about anyone (even after his totally unfair sacking from Thames Television in 1990) and he was greatly loved by all who knew him. It goes without saying, too, that to work with him was a joy of equal proportion and it is with the deepest respect and greatest love that I devote this chapter to the memory of a great man of comedy.

I first met Benny in 1959, initially through his great friend Peter Charlesworth, and our friendship was re-ignited when he gave us his vocal support (and a sausage roll) during my cabaret appearances with Lionel Blair. Throughout the sixties – as the Ladybirds – we appeared occasionally on the 'Benny Hill Show' but from 1969 until his untimely death in 1992, we worked with him solidly. If we had respect for Benny, he had the greatest of respect for us as a vocal group and it was little surprise to him when we were voted best vocal group by the New Musical Express in 1970 – due, almost entirely, to our work on television. His attitude was one of complete faith in our professional work and most times, when he gave us the music parts to sing, he would start off by looking to describe the way he wanted it done and, seconds later, would throw his hands in the air and say "Oh – you know what I mean – just do it!!" And you know something?.....we did and Benny was always delighted. It was always fun and Benny had us continually creased up with laughter.

He would walk into the rehearsal room carrying, not a briefcase or an expensive leather attaché case, but a branded plastic shopping bag advertising a well known supermarket containing his sandwiches for lunch and any groceries he had purchased on the way. He would hope we would not notice him but we always did. We would run over to him and surround him.

"Hiya – Ben" we would say in greeting, pursing our lips forward to kiss him.

"Just the one" he would reply "one only!"

His weight was a great problem to him and it seemed he was always on a diet but what a laugh we'd all have when we caught him out, nibbling a biscuit or worse. I recall him telling me quite seriously, that he was a glutton in the real meaning of the word. If he was having a meal of fish fingers and chips, for instance, (his favourite!) he would only purchase a small frozen packet of each, for to buy the larger ones, would result in him cooking and eating the lot. He just did not have the will power to use up a reasonable portion and put the remainder back in the freezer. Benny's favourite line by way of argument was to say *"Will power? I have plenty of will power! The trouble is – I haven't any won't power!!"* Alfred, his father, must take some blame for this excess for he had always instilled in the boys' minds that 'being large is a sign of prosperity'. If that had been the case, then Benny's brother Leonard must have been very rich when he died for his weight, by then, had surpassed 23 stone.

Benny was mischievous, gentle, shy and petrified of females – hard to believe when you watch his shows but true, nonetheless. He was very fond of us but when a reporter asked the question during an interview what he thought about us always working with him and why did he always choose us?, he replied –

"Well, first of all, I think of ... the Supremes!" His face broke into a crooked grin, then into a wicked smile.

"If they're not available – then I think of the Supremes" His grin was now an evil leer – his trademark!

"And if I can't get them – I think of the Ladybirds!!" He *always* ended up with us, I'm glad to say, for not only did we sing the vocal backing out of vision but we were also heavily featured *in* vision with Benny, singing all the wonderful comedy ditties, (which, incidentally, he wrote himself), and on many occasions performing our own vocal spot. We were lucky, lucky girls and we knew it! Spending so much time with Benny, it was inevitable that, when he was asked to put on disc his many funny songs, we joined him in the studios to provide the vocal backing. Listen to his No. 1 hit 'Ernie (the fastest milkman in the West!)' and the female backing singers you hear behind him is us – The Ladybirds.

The aforementioned sacking of this comedy genius from Thames Television hurt him more than we'll ever know and all those close to him swear that his unfair dismissal contributed to the cause of his death a few yeas later – a heart attack whilst watching television. Two months before he died we, and all those who worked on the show, were attending the funeral of Ted Taylor, a musical associate of Benny's and the comic was in sombre mood – unusual for him. "I suppose none of us last for ever" he mused "makes you think, though". He was unnerved, I suppose, by the fact that Ted was younger than him and the implication bothered him. On the brighter side, however, was the signing of a new contract with Central TV to do the 'Benny Hill Show' for the next five years – at the ratio of four shows a year. And, of course, lovely, loyal Benny had insisted on the Ladybirds. (The Supremes were still not available!) Before leaving Benny on that sad occasion, I gave him a big hug and a kiss on his cheek "Thanks for that, Ben" I said "I need the money". Benny blushed and looked embarrassed. Incredibly, to this day, we still receive repeat fees from all over the world and from countries you would least expect. Today – I received a cheque from Estonia for £31.20 and that, in itself, is its own tribute to a comedy great.

If Benny was idolised in Great Britain, he was no less thought of in America. Even today when I visit the States on holiday and word leaks out that I had some connection with the 'Benny Hill Show' – I am treated like royalty – such is the awe, respect and high regard the American public hold for the comic. It matters not that I was a singer on the show and a personal friend of the star – if I had been the tea lady or his personal toilet cleaner, the result would have been the same.

"Gee honey, she actually *knew* Benny Hill" – instant magic!! The great stars from across the pond also idolise our comedy hero. Clint Eastwood, the rugged veteran of the 'Dirty Harry' films, plus a thousand more, now owns a restaurant in his home town of Cartmel, California and the décor is a shrine to Benny – photographs, posters, record covers and much more, cover the walls in tribute.

Frank Sinatra, another great admirer, flew into Heathrow for a series of concerts and told the waiting press "I have two ambitions whilst in Britain. One is to sing with the Royal Philharmonic Orchestra and the other is to meet Benny Hill and watch a rehearsal".

Probably the most bizarre accolade, however, was the arrival of Michael Jackson at the London hospital where Benny was recovering from his first heart attack. He was a great fan of the show and an even bigger fan of Benny himself. He instructed that his visit was to remain a secret to the staff and public alike but his idea of a secret was a million miles from anyone else's. Like a scene from the 'Godfather' movie, the entourage arrived in a fleet of black limousines, with darkened windows hiding the occupants from view. Six massive black bodyguards alighted and spaced themselves along the corridor, daring anyone to move. Michael appeared, flanked by another two mafia 'look-alikes' and made his way to Benny's room, hoping that his arrival had gone without being noticed! The two great stars spent the next two hours wrapped in each other's company with Benny doing most of the talking for Michael was too busy rolling on the floor laughing hysterically and wiping the tears from his eyes. He promised Benny that the next film he made, would feature a special part in it for him to play (something that Benny would have adored) but it never came to pass. Had it happened however – we may have seen one of the greatest comedy double acts of all time. What a thought!

During his career Benny received many awards for his TV programmes and especially, his contributions to comedy. By far the most important to him, however, was the highly prestigious 'Charlie Chaplin Award for Comedy' for Charlie had been his idol all his life. Indeed Benny, at the age of three, has amused friends and family alike with his impersonation of the 'Charlie Chaplin' walk To receive the award (very few of these are ever given) Benny travelled to Switzerland, accompanied by his friend and TV show director Dennis Kirkland and was thrilled to be given the prize by Eugene Chaplin, son of the great comedian. Even better was to follow, for they were invited back to the family home and into Charlie's study where Eugene pointed out the chair and the televsion set where the great man had sat watching the 'Benny Hill Show', roaring with laughter. On the wall by his side, was a shelf laden with video tapes of Benny and Eugene, pointing at them, said "My Father thought you were the greatest!" At that, Benny cried.

Even though this was the proudest moment of his life, Benny remained the modest, thoughtful and kind person he had always been and looked to praise others who had contributed to his success. On receiving the beautiful, golden silhouette of Charlie, he turned to Dennis and handed it to him.. "I want you to have this" he said "You deserve this as much, if not more, than I." Dennis was stunned but accepted the gesture and I was so thrilled to see, on a very recent visit to his home, that the priceless statuette has pride of place for all to view.

Benny Hill died on Easter Saturday 18th April 1992 at the age of 68. The funeral was held in his home town of Southampton and with heavy, heavy heart I, and the other Ladybirds, drove to Benny's home to deliver a giant floral ladybird, before joining the cortège heading to the cemetery. The weather was dark and dismal and the mood seemed to envelope the whole city. The roads were closed to all traffic and the thousands who lined the route wore an air of sadness and grief. We reached Benny's final resting place and grouped ourselves around the grave. Just as the coffin was being lowered into the ground, as if on cue, the heavens opened and the rain poured down in a torrent. Dennis Kirkland, Benny's best friend and Producer/Director of the show shouted "Ben would love this. He would appreciate the timing" then he added "And you know what? – I'll bet that bugger's sitting on a cloud holding a giant hosepipe, soaking us all and laughing his bloody head off!" Somehow the thought softened the moment and we laughed through our tears. On one of the saddest days of my life, there was an even sadder moment for us all when we realised that our darling Bob Todd, who had worked with Benny so often and so brilliantly in the comedy sketches, had not made the funeral but when he later told us the reason, we began to believe more and more, that Benny was looking down on us all and, with his wicked sense of humour, enjoying himself thoroughly.

Bob Todd lived in Sussex and had arranged to meet up with co-stars Henry McGee and Jon Jon Keefe at Maidenhead before travelling the rest of the way by car. Bob set out to catch his train and on the way, arranged to call into Moss Bros in London to pick up his formal suit (Bob *never* wore formal clothes and so didn't own one!) The stop-over took longer than expected and after a taxi dash to Paddington Station, he rushed to the wrong platform. Luck, for now, was on his side and he eventually made the train he had planned and he sat back in his seat, congratulating himself on having completed his part of the journey, successfully. Pride came before a fall, however, and fate (or perhaps Benny) decided he had gone far enough. Within sight of Maidenhead Station, the train ground to a halt and refused to move for 20 minutes. Bob fumed and cursed but to no avail with the result that, by the time he finally arrived at the meeting point, Henry and Jon Jon had gone without him. He was distraught and decided to do the next best thing – retire to the nearest pub and get 'rat-arsed'. Bob toasted Benny and kept on doing so until he fell over – our Benny, we are sure, toasted him back.

Before finishing this chapter on Benny, let me relate to you one of Benny's stories – I know he won't mind! Early on in his career, he auditioned for the American film producer – Blake Edwards (husband of Julie Andrews). The part was very small – playing the role of a French waiter. When Benny was directed to speak in French, he replied "Would you like a Paris accent..... East side or West? Perhaps I should do someone from the South of France or what about Marseille? How about Carmargue?" Blake Edwards was not impressed. "Mr Hill" he said "Everyone hates a 'smart-ass!" and he promptly kicked him out. Benny, however, was *not* being boastful and certainly would not have played any such game – he was too honest and too shy. It just so happens that he was fluent in French with all its regional accents, in addition to Spanish, Italian and German. What a talent! He was surely a man with the face and body of a clown and the brain of a genius.

There will never be another !

Rest in peace, dear Benny

CHAPTER 16

My Annus Horribilis!

Work had gradually lessened during the late 80's but everything came to a head as I entered the new year of 1988 – the year I called my Annus Horribilis. It was a dreadful twelve months for me (and my family) and I pray to God I never have to suffer another like it. On the first of January – New Year's Day – my dear Mum died. It was a dreadful shock to us all, but the pain I was suffering at her passing was not helped by the cracks that were now appearing in my marriage, and in February of that awful year, I began divorce proceedings and our house was put up for sale.

I began looking for somewhere suitable to live, along with Anna and Paul and we eventually found a property that looked ideal. In October, we finally moved in but even that was filled with the dramas that seem to go with the exercise. I will not bore you with the details but, suffice to say, when we eventually took ownership of the property, we were drained and frustrated and near to screaming point. If it appeared we had finally turned the corner, then more was to come – for the year ended as tragically as it had begun when, on December 7th, my darling Dad died. To lose both one's parents, one's husband and one's home in the space of twelve nightmare months is a body blow so difficult to bear but, thankfully my Aunt Liz and Uncle Ernie came down from Birkenhead for the festive season and their warmth and wonderful sense of 'Scouse' humour at least put a smile back on our faces, but we longed for the new year to begin and what we hoped would be a new beginning.

CHAPTER 17

The Vernons Girls reform .... for Cliff Richard!!

It *was* a new beginning, as if in apology for the sorrow the last year had contained. It began with a phone call. I love phone calls and this time, I had a premonition that the news awaiting me was going to be good. I picked up the phone and the voice said – 'Maggie Stredder? Oh, Hi! This is Cliff Richard's office here. We're doing two shows at Wembley Stadium in June to commemorate Cliff's thirty years in showbiz. We're calling it 'THE EVENT' and it will last for around five hours. In the first hour, Cliff wants to re-create the fabulous 'Oh Boy Show' which started off his career. Can you get the Vernon's Girls together again for the show?" I felt a surge of excitement, tinged with some doubt.

'Well" I explained "I'm obviously in touch with the girls but only five of us stayed in show business and the rest returned home to get married and have families. I don't know what shape they are in – some could still be slim but others will probably be skinny or even fat – I don't know".

"Don't worry" came the reply "Cliff realises this and doesn't mind whatever their shapes. He still wants them, so will you let me know?"

That was all I wanted to hear. For the next few days, my telephone almost melted as I made contact with all the girls once again. I explained to each one in turn what Cliff had said and exactly what he required. "So how do you feel about coming down to London for two weeks, staying in a hotel together like old times, learning the music, learning the dance routines, meeting up with everyone and working with Cliff – oh, and would you mind leaving behind your husbands to do the housework and the baby-sitting?"

"Yes! Yes! Yes!" they yelled back at me to a Vernons Girl and that is exactly what we did. It was an absolute joy. I taught the girls the numbers and the vocal backing we were to do and a gorgeous young choreographer took us through the dance routines. He really was quite a hunk, with legs that went on for ever (apparently he holds the record of the longest legs for a male ballet dancer) and we let him know, in no uncertain terms, that he was making twelve middle aged ladies feel very young again. We gave him such a hard time but he took it in good spirit (I guess he really didn't have much choice!). I was still a Vernons Girl short and had no hesitation in asking Penny Lightfoot, my pal, fellow session singer and fellow Ladybird to join. She was delighted to do so and fitted the role perfectly.

The two weeks of rehearsal were such fun and the girls sang and moved just as well as they had forty two years earlier! We couldn't wait, however, for the big day(s) to arrive – 16th and 17th June 1989 – and we prayed that the weather would not spoil the event. We need not have worried for both nights were warm and balmy – ideal for the concert that was, despite the wonderful television and stage shows we had done in the past, the highlight of our career. The perfect weather only confirmed what I already knew – that Cliff has a hot line to God!! If the show topped anything the Vemons Girls had done in the past, I believe that Cliff felt the same way and as 'curtain up' drew near, the atmosphere was electric. Sharing the stage on these two memorable evenings were, of course, The Shadows, The Kalin Twins, Gerry and The Pacemakers, Cathy McGowan, The Searchers, Aswad, The Dallas Boys, the 'Oh Boy' Band, The Vernons Girls, compere Jimmy Henney (as on the original 'Oh Boy' show) and for the big finale, standing high above us all on a huge podium, stood Cliff, resplendent in a sparkling white suit. It was sensational stuff and at a given point, the entire audience (over 70,000) lit up their pre-supplied throwaway torches to create an effect so breathtaking that we all ended up in tears and, if truth be known and honesty prevails, we were not the only ones – by far!

The Vernons Girls – or at least the majority, returned to Liverpool but we down here descended into a pall of gloom , such was the anti climax following the great heights we had reached – but the feeling was not to last long, for me, at any rate.

CHAPTER 18

Getting our act together – times three

Once again, a phone call – this time from Sheila (the ex Vernons Girl who had gone solo with great success and won 'New Faces').

"Maggie – how do you fancy starting a trio as the Vernons Girls?" Of course, I was interested.

"Tell me more" I said and she explained that a small time impresario had phoned her, bemoaning the fact that all the male 'wrinklies' from the 60's were back on the road strutting their stuff but there simply weren't enough females from that era. "He's suggested we reform as a trio for he is preparing a tour of over 70 one-nighters, and it's ours if we want it!" Sheila then asked how I felt about it and I thought – why not? It could be fun. We agreed that the third girl should be Penny Lightfoot and because work was becoming a little thin on the ground, she accepted – happily! Penny's background is one of the highest quality. She was born in Yorkshire. (Her Mum still lives in Hunnanby, near Filey and the main reason for telling you this is because, whenever we work in that area, she becomes our Landlady – the best 'digs' imaginable with food 'to die for'! If you send me a stamped addressed envelope and a small cheque to cover my commission, I'll give you her address!) As you know, I have known Penny for many years as a free-lance session singer with a wonderful alto voice and she has worked with the very best including the famous vocal group The Mike Sammes Singers. She has provided vocal backing for many of the 'greats' including Barbra Streisand, Charles Aznavour and particularly, Petula Clark with whom she toured worldwide, before becoming a Ladybird 'proper' in 1984.

So there I was, with two pals, about to embark on another roller coaster ride of one-night stands, long car journeys and food from motorway service station restaurants and 'greasy spoon' cafeterias. What swayed me, however, apart from the excitement of re-creating the musical sounds of the late 50's and 60's, was the fact that both Sheila and Penny were highly experienced and quality performers who had seen it all, done it all and lived to tell the tale. I felt that with the combination of all our talents put together, the overall presentation would be one that would do justice to the very name we chose to revive – The Vernons Girls.

We informed the promoter of our decision and lost no time in getting our act together, organising the music and the costumes. How exciting – 45 years of age and a new career beckoning! Sharing the bill with us was Wee Willie Harris, Don Lang, Terry Dene, Tommy Bruce, Jet Harris and Pete Murray (who else) and we set out to take the UK by storm. The show was called '6-5 Special'. It was an unmitigated disaster! We had begged constantly for the list of tour dates and had always been 'fobbed off' with the excuse – 'just a few more dates to fill and we'll send it'. A few more dates? You must be joking! Of the seventy plus dates offered, we only did four and only got paid for one! Well – I hear you say – that's show business ! – and it is, but with our experience, we should have known better! We had spent a great deal on stage- wear and good quality music arrangements and rather than see it all go up in smoke, we decided to carry on. We phoned everyone we knew, agents, managers and bookers – and gradually the work started to come in and the more it did, the more we loved it.

In 1991 we embarked on a tour of the Pontin Holiday Centres situated on the South Coast of England. It consisted of five evenings per week , a different Centre each night plus two days off, before starting the same run again. This contract was to run for a total of three months – 60 shows in all and had been arranged for us by Jim Kennedy, Pontins Entertainment Executive – great stuff !. We were impressed by this gentle, unassuming man who knew absolutely all there is to know about entertainment and probably a bit more and, although we saw little of him during the period, we spoke occasionally by phone. Little did I realise then, that we would meet up again in February 1998 and that he would have such a dramatic and emotional effect on my life – but that was to come.

The season with Pontins gave us our appetite for this type of work, for the audiences were a delight. The Centres were divided into two distinct categories – Family Centres for the younger parents with children and Golden Breaks for the older clientele, who look for a more peaceful and laid-back holiday. We performed at the latter and the audiences revelled in the nostalgic melodies, reliving their memories of the magical 50's/60's. Of course, we 'sent' ourselves up just a little and this endeared us to the guests even more. Everywhere we went we got standing ovations and needless to say, we loved every second. We worked, too, for Butlins and

Haven but our special favourite was, and still is, the Warner Adult Centres. Each is either a former stately home or castle and the atmosphere is one of elegance and gentility. The bands are always of the highest quality and we are welcomed by the staff like members of their own family. If you haven't been there, please, please treat yourself. You won't be disappointed. With the number of theatres in this country still diminishing and the club scene becoming a thing of the past (especially for cabaret artistes), the Holiday Centres continue to keep our business flourishing and our date book healthy.

Another area for providing work is the booming cruise market and in 1996 we were invited to join the P & O Liner 'The Canberra' for a 'themed' cruise – celebrating the Swinging Sixties. Working with us for the two week period, was the brilliant Craig Douglas ('She Was Only Sixteen'), the lovely Jess Conrad ('Mystery Girl') Pete Murray and our own backing band, Rockin' Horse. It proved a wonderful combination of sunshine, good food and performing to a captive audience (nobody leaves the ship when we're on!) who are all Sixties fans` anyway – a joy!

If that was to prove a highlight then even better was to come for during that same year we were invited by Hal Carter and tour promoters, Flying Music, to be a part of a three and a half month tour of the United

Three 'jolly tars' on the P & O 'Canberra' – Sheila, Maggie & Penny

Kingdom in a show to be called 'The Solid Gold Rock'n'Roll show'. The show was to co-star Joe Brown & the Bruvvers and Marty Wilde and the Wildcats along with Eden Kane and John Leyton. The backing band was again Rockin' Horse, led by the shy, retiring drummin' man Mac Poole (who's kidding who?). The tour proved to be an incredible success. Everywhere we went, and that included the London Palladium, the business was phenomenal. 'Sold out' notices outside the theatres and concert halls became the norm and the audiences were fantastic. Without exception, they were all fans of that era and the atmosphere was electric. The show always started with an overture from 'Rockin' Horse' and an off-stage introduction brought on the Vernons Girls. First act on? The worst spot in the show, when the audiences are not yet warmed up, unresponsive and unfriendly? Not on your life! The excitement pre-show had built up to such a crescendo, our appearance ignited the blue touch paper and the place exploded. Are you ready to rock'n'roll? They certainly were and they let us know it! Such was the success of the show and such was the great camaraderie between all of us who took part (and I include not just the performers on stage but the light and sound engineers and the stage crews who slave tirelessly behind the scenes without the credit they deserve), that we have embarked on a further four tours – with an eighteen month gap between each tour – with the same line up. It is such fun to do and if we give pleasure to the thousands of fans who come to see the show – let me tell you, it is nothing to the thrill their very presence gives us. The appreciation and love which pour from the masses in the auditorium is a joy to all of us. It is a bond between us and such a warm lovely feeling to know that none of us has been forgotten. Thank you all for your loyal support – we love you!

CHAPTER 19

The fourth Vernons Girl – Lily Savage!

Throughout my life, the telephone has become a friend. Yes – I do realise that, at times, it can convey devastating or tragic news but, in my case, thankfully, its cheery ring more often than not, brings something to savour. In this case, it was a cheery voice, rich in the flavour of Liverpool – unmistakably Paul O'Grady. Perhaps you've never heard of him? Think back, therefore, to my childhood days in Birkenhead when I, through no choice of mine, had to wear the cast off clothes of my two male cousins and I talked of a near neighbour who 'cross dressed' in the other direction to become a popular TV star. Now you've got it!! The call was from Lily Savage!

In the early days, Paul in the guise of his alter-ego, had stormed the clubs and pubs performing a mime act, using taped recordings of all the well known female singers around at that time. One of the most popular was the Vernons Girls 'Funny all Over' which was made in 1963 on the Decca Label and stayed in the charts for 8 weeks. Paul had never forgotten how well that number had gone and, after having agreed with BBC TV to host a series of 'The Lily Savage Show', he invited us to be one of the guest stars. He wanted us to sing a medley of songs attributed to us, including 'Funny all Over' and 'You Know What I Mean' (another chart entry for four weeks). In that nasal 'Scouse' accent, so familiar, he said "Y'see Maggie, I always desperately wanted to be a Vernons Girl – and now's me chance!", the idea being that we would wear the 'hot pants' outfits with the tight tops which carried our individual names emblazoned across the chest, and he would join us, in similar costume. The result was wonderful television and whilst we had worked hard at keeping our figures and, particularly our legs, in good shape, he outshone us all. His figure was gorgeous and where he hid the 'dangly bits' is anyone's guess. I wonder if he's free for the next 'Solid Gold' tour?

*I share a relaxing
moment with
Cliff Richard*

*The Vernons Girls reformed for 'The Event' show at Wembley Stadium.
With the Dallas boys*

'The Event' plays to 140,000 fans – incredible!!

"No, Cliff, I want you to do it my way!"

Never work with animals...! I provide the 'voice' on TV for superdog – Schnorbitz

The Vernons Girls today – Maggie, Sheila & Penny

'The Solid Gold Rock'n'roll Show' (L to R) Back row: – Marty Wilde, The Vernons Girls and Joe Brown Front row: – John Leyton & Eden Kane

To The FaBulous 'VERNONS' FROM a life long Fan who Finally Fulfilled an ambition much love & respect Paul/xx

Above:
A kind and thoughtful note of thanks
from Lily Savage (otherwise known as
Paul O'Grady) after the TV show

Left: The lovely 'boy turned girl' –
Lily Savage

Lily becomes the fourth Vernons girl on the 'Lily Savage Show'
(This photograph was taken from the TV screen during the show
– hence the slight distortion)

One final footnote from that particular show, was the conversation we had in the 'Green Room' after the show. Paul was telling me about his hosting of the TV game show 'Blankety Blank' "It's great fun" he said "and I enjoy doing it – but the bloody signature tune drives me insane".

"Well" I replied "you'd better get to love it, for its making me a lot of money!" Paul hadn't realised that the vocals on that particular number were the voices of the Ladybirds (as they were on many other signature tunes, including 'Hi-de-Hi!') Well – we have to make a living somehow!

Before finishing this chapter, let me pick up on the closing lines of the last paragraph and explain that in addition to the hundreds of shows we did as a solo act in our own right, The Ladybirds were always in the recording studios singing the many signature tunes we still hear today, plus dozens of advertising jingles still recognised by those old enough to remember. Today, I spend many an enjoyable evening giving talks on my 'show business life' and when I mention the jingles, I spend a fun 15 minutes giving them the first line of the 'ditty' and asking them to sing the rest. I can't believe how many complete the course. Let me list a few of the best known jingles we made and see how many you remember ?

The   Esso   Sign   Means   ....?

(Heinz Beans) – Pick up ....?

(Camay Soap) – You'll look ....?

(Comfort) – Softness is ....?

Boom! Boom! Boom! Boom! ....?

Opal Fruits – made ....?

Murraymints, Murraymints – too ....?

(Fairy Liquid) – Now hands ....?

John Collier, John Collier – The ....?

There you are! Anyone scoring a maximum of 10/10 is either as old as me, or lying about their age – no comment please!

CHAPTER 20

Singing, Talking.............and Jim.

In 1997,with work becoming spasmodic and irregular, certainly not enough to rely on for a living, I began to look at other ways to augment my earnings from the Vernons Girls. When someone mentioned that I should give talks on my life in show business (should, of course, anyone be interested!) I sat up and took notice. It was suggested that Women's' Clubs would be the ideal venues for the subject and, with this mind, I sat down to write my story. It wasn't as easy as I had imagined for, when you reach the age of 45, the memory begins to go, but I jotted down most of the highlights, condensing it into a one hour presentation – the usual time allowed. Well – I now had the story but where do I take it? Where do I start?

The Women's Institutes came to mind and I wrote off to the Surrey Branch – the nearest to where I lived. They immediately offered me an audition but to my disappointment, it was not for another six months, so, undeterred I carried on writing furiously (and frustratingly) to every club I could think of.

A chance meeting in my local Building Society proved the breakthrough I was looking for. Her name was Sylvia Fowler and, for many years, had been in charge of the restaurants and bars at Thames Television. She was, without doubt, instrumental in the 'Ladybirds' being treated as honoured guests whenever we crossed the threshold into the hallowed halls of the studios – our beloved place of work. Everyone, from the floor crews to the major stars (including Benny Hill who, on more than one occasion, left her a £50 tip!), adored her and she and her staff treated each person in the same way – with respect and kindness.

We chatted for a long while (not difficult), each catching up with the other's news and what we were currently doing with our lives. And so it came to pass that – lo and behold – she informed me that she was – and still is – Treasurer of a Club , 'The Eight o'Clock Circle Ladies Group'. I was amazed at the hand that Fate had dealt me and told her of my new venture.

"You get your talk ready" she said "and I will ring you with a definite booking to appear at our Club". True to her word, she 'phoned as promised and on Thursday 7th May 1998, I stepped out in front of a live audience (not without nerves!) to present my story. It went well and the ladies seemed to enjoy it – I know I did.

My audition with the W.I. was also in May and, to be honest, I *almost* enjoyed it. Auditions are always nerve wracking experiences and this was no exception but I do recall telling the hundred or so ladies in the audience that this was only the second audition I had attended, ever. The first, with the Vernons Girls, turned out, for me at least, to be a moment of destiny and which changed my life for ever......but I'll tell you about that in a moment! The W.I. talk went very well and my new career began to snowball to the extent that now I am not only on their speakers list for W.I.s but am included in the lists for clubs affiliated to the National Association of Women's Clubs, throughout the South East corner of England. I am asked to do charity lunches, after-dinners plus other functions and I love it – almost as much as singing with the Vernons Girls!! The success of the talk prompted many clubs to ask for return engagements and, of course, not being able to repeat my'show business' story, I set out to write a second, "My Benny Hill Story" and a third, "My Max Bygraves Story (with Singalong)." A fourth is in the pipeline. Exciting stuff and great fun to do!

Happily, this new direction has never interfered with the Vernons Girls work and the two compliment each other. In February 1998 – this is the story is promised you!! – we were asked to headline a showcase (posh name for an audition) at a hotel in the Midlands being organised by Studio One, a Theatrical Agency based in Coventry, for their clients, Holiday Club Pontins. We were not happy about doing it for we had worked for Pontins in the past and felt that they knew of us already. We were 'soft-soaped', however, into believing that the 'headliners' were not auditioning – merely providing a professional finish to the evening and after such flattery, what could we do, but accept? Fate decreed, however, that we were meant to be there! We convinced ourselves that maybe other agents might be there and the opportunity to be seen was a possibility, so we made our way North for the show. (Remember, auditions mean that you don't get paid to appear *and* you have to pay your own expenses!) We were pleasantly surprised to see our dear friend Jim Kennedy there, in charge of the proceedings, – although we shouldn't have been – and before long, we were enjoying a cup of tea in his company. Such a nice man, who, you will recall gave us that wonderful summer season touring the Pontin Centres on the South Coast. Jim and I chatted at every opportunity during the evening and, without doubt, we both felt the chemistry that existed. Nevertheless, we did the job that was asked and, despite the late hour – it was somewhere near 1.00 a.m. before we took the stage – the audience stayed up and gave us a great reception.

Two weeks later, there was a message on my answer-phone from 'Gentleman Jim', as he was known in the business, asking me to ring him. At first I thought it could be the offer of more work but when he added that if I missed him at the office, "here's my home telephone number in Blackpool", I began to wonder, and hope, that, perhaps, it was personal. Well – I *did* ring him at home, at 4 o'clock on the Saturday afternoon – and it lasted for over 3 hours! That set the pattern for the next few months and we rang each other constantly – each call lasting no less that the very first. Our phone bills were astronomical! A lovely, warm, intimate courtship, courtesy of Alexander Graham Bell.

In May, Jim travelled, as he usually did, visiting the Centres now opening for the summer season, to the South Coast and on the way home, he broke his journey and took me out to dinner. We talked and talked and held hands and when he kissed me later in the evening, I knew it was becoming serious. Every week end from then on, Jim made the journey to my home, returning to work (near Preston) either Sunday evening or Monday morning, a round trip of nearly 500 miles and our courtship continued to deepen. It flourished throughout the summer and in October 1998 we decided to take a holiday in Florida (God forbid – Jim needed one after all that driving!) One day, after a tiring morning soaking up the sun, we retired after lunch, to enjoy an afternoon nap. Neither of us could sleep, however, and we got up to pour ourselves a drink. Jim had a strange look in his eye and to my amazement – and joy – he suddenly dropped onto bended knee ..... and proposed! At his age it was an unwise thing to do but I helped him back onto his feet – and accepted.

We were married on the 17th April 1999 at the Surbiton Methodist Church – me wearing a slinky red lace number and Jim, being Scottish, resplendent in the kilt. Most of the males attending also wore the tartan and it was a wonderful, colourful day. It rained all the morning but when I arrived at the church, the sun shone from a blue sky. As soon as we arrived at the reception and sat down for the meal and speeches, the rains came back with a vengeance. It was surely meant to be. My lovely daughter Anna and grand daughter Charlotte were bridesmaids and my handsome son Paul, gave me away (I think he was rather relieved to get rid of me!) Jim's brother Ian was best man and during the reception, in which the Vernons Girls(naturally) performed the cabaret, it was great to turn the clock back to the 'Oh Boy' days and welcome that great performer Vince Eager, as a special surprise. He sang for the guests and his voice is as good as – or even better, than before. We honeymooned in Hawaii – fantastic!

After all the excitement, Jim had to journey back to the North West of England to work and so, yet again, we had to endure only seeing each other at week ends. Happily for me, however, Jim decided to take retirement in December 1999 – just in time for the last leg (in Scotland) of the 'Solid Gold' Rock'n'Roll tour. Jim came with us for the last few weeks

Jim & I tie the knot, April 17th, 1999

and helped us by taking over as driver – a big relief for, after three and a half months on the road, we were exhausted. The tour finished in December at the London Palladium and was considered, as always, a huge success. We looked forward to the next one (possibly the last?) in eighteen months time. Finally, Jim and I were able to settle down to a more normal (what's normal?) existence.

Jim, fulfilling a long held ambition, began writing his autobiography in 2000 called "One Good Turn Deserves an Encore" and it was published, by Showbiz Publications, on 1st June 2001. As Head of Pontins Entertainment for 32 years. plus his years in variety and a term as Cruise Director on the P & O Liners *Arcadia* & *Canberra*, he has a lot of great stories to tell – almost as many as I have! It was he who, after realising that my story had been written, suggested he tidy it up and translate it from my native 'Scouse' (plus indeterminate scribbles and jottings,) into the more understandable English you are reading now!

The one thing now that is missing in our lives is a new family. Everyone is anxiously awaiting the news of an impending happy event but, being the sensible people we are, have decided to wait a few years longer in order to know each other better, before booking the stork! That's only common sense, is it not?

So, my friends (I feel I can call you that if you're still reading this book!) I feel very fortunate to have had

Daughter Anna, son Paul & grand daughter Charlotte on my wedding day, 17th April, 1999

such an extremely joyful and successful career. I feel blessed, too, in having met Jim so late in my life (45) and in being so happy. I am well known for continually saying "My singers and I – both male *and* female – have had more laughs than anyone is entitled to have in this life". This still holds true today. Another 'Solid Gold' tour is in hand and my diary is full-to-bursting with talks, well into next year and beyond. If, and when, the Vernons Girls decide to hang up their 'short shorts', I can continue performing and writing, recalling more great days working with the stars of recording and TV fame and if I am blessed with good health and can keep on for another 10 years, that will make me a very happy and contented lady of ...... years of age!!!

Anyone want to borrow a calculator?

REFLECTIONS

My book is finished.

I have spent the last few days proofing it for mistakes in spelling and in grammar and it is now with the printers. I am resting. I close my eyes but can see nothing but commas, full stops and exclamation marks. Nevertheless, I am relaxed - yet still the memories of my life wash over me, evoking warm thoughts of people and places, of events and occasions. I feel the need to write them down as they pass through my head – in no specific order but simply to record the importance of the moment, as it happened. Perhaps you will allow me this one, final indulgence.

For my book is now finished.!

* Paul & Linda McCartney record an album as Wings. We, the Ladybirds, provide the vocal backing. Paul gently pulls Linda away from our microphone.

  "Leave the girls alone, Linda" he says. "They're doin' all right on their own. They don't need you – and y'know you can't sing, anyway!"

* Bumping into Elton (John) at the height of his fame, coming out of the lift at the BBC. "Hi'ya Maggie" he shouts loudly, "How are you? Say, how about us meeting up one day soon and swapping some 'specs'?" Great guy – he never forgets a face!

* Tom Jones, in the 80's, at the Pebble Mill Studio in Birmingham. He sees me half way down the corridor. "Bloody Hell, Maggie" he yells after me "Your not *still* at it, are you?" What a cheek," says I. "What's good for the Welsh goose is just as good for the 'Scouse' gander" ... !

* The early Ladybirds (just Glo and I) appear on 'Thank Your Lucky Stars' and have to calm down a singer, frozen with nerves and

trembling with fear. His knees are knocking. Yes – him again! You wouldn't think it of Tom Jones, would you?

* In the middle of a 'Glen Campbell' series, I am suffering and badly swollen with mumps. I wear a long muffler wound round and round my neck and turn up at the studios to work. Very naughty of me, for I could infect everyone in the show. I just cannot turn down work and, in any event, I adore Glen Campbell. I met him in Branson a couple of years ago, so sure he will be thrilled to see me. Sadly, he doesn't have a clue who I am. Perhaps he doesn't recognise me without the swellings on my neck. That must be the reason!

* Vic Damone asking me for a date – and him still married to Pier Angeli!!! Dear! Dear!

* The wonderful recordings for 'Holiday On Ice' – the show which travels the world. We never skate but we pre-record all the music with my wonderful bunch of talented singers. They can sing anything and 'cover' (impersonate) any one you can name. Joan Baxter – famous for the voices of Marilyn Monroe, Judy Garland, Cleo Laine, Gracie Fields and still in great demand today for her own glorious voice.

* Ken Barrie, the voice of Postman Pat, who also sings as Perry Como, Frank Sinatra, Tony Bennett and Nat 'King' Cole. Danny Street and Mike Redway, who you hear regularly on BBC radio as soloists and with the Maggie Stredder Singers on all my recordings and when male voices are needed. Gosh! They're good ... Thanks guys!!

* The Ladybirds own solo albums plus 'The Ladybirds Sing the Hits of 1977' and 'The Ladybirds Go Country'. Didn't take the world by storm but we loved recording them. I am very proud of them.

* So proud, too, of our voices on the signature tune of 'Chance in a Million' starring Simon Callow. The music is arranged by Ronnie Aldrich and we have to read it on sight. I think I am more proud of that than any other single piece of work we have done. The song is entitled 'Taking a Chance on Love'

* Peggy Lee on a TV show. She has put on a lot of weight and her voice has gone. She is in a wheelchair. Her face is the stiffest and most wrinkle-free I have ever seen. My heart goes out to her.

* The Three Degrees, at the height of their fame. They do their very first TV show in the UK on the 'Des O'Connor Show'. They are shellshocked at meeting the Ladybirds! "I must have a photo taken with you for my daughter" Sheila Ferguson trills. "Her 'street-cred' will rocket when she shows the photo to her friends. *My* Mother with the famous Ladybirds ... *from the Benny Hill Show !!*" I ask you. It is moments like this that stop you from being big-headed!!!

* Again the 'Des O'Connor Show'. The Everley Brothers make a bee-line for the Ladybirds. Phil speaks. "I want to thank you for all the joy you have given us ... *on The Benny Hill Show!!!!*" No comment!

* Yet again, the 'Des O'Connor Show'. Joan Rivers, who became quite a regular, walks past us in the corridor and hisses "You're rubbish!! We are devastated but it is only her sense of humour – and we become great pals!!

My love and eternal thanks to all my dear pals, past and present.

What a lucky girl I am!!

APPENDIX

Recordings made with –

Sandie Shaw

Dusty Springfield

Shirley Bassey

Lulu

Clodagh Rogers

Tom Jones

Walker Brothers

Long John Baldry

Wayne Fontana

Jimmi Hendrix

Engelbert Humperdinck

Beatles

Wings

Benny Hill

Cat Stevens

Hurricane Smith

Dana

Lena Martell

Lena Zavaroni

Rolf Harris

Cilla Black

Paul Jones

Mantovani

Paul Nicholas

Rod Stewart

Cliff Richard

Demis Roussos

Frankie Vaughan

Des O'Connor

Ken Dodd

Bing Crosby

Fred Astaire

Jack Jones

Gene Pitney

Olivia Newton-John

The Bachelors

Television Shows (Series)

Sooty

Crackerjack

Simon Dee

Les Dawson

Two Ronnies

Morecambe & Wise

Little & Large

Glen Campbell

Wednesday at Eight

Children in Need

London Night Out

Golden Shot

Tommy Cooper

Harry Worth

Sandie Shaw

Paul Daniels

Generation Game

Shirley Bassey

Jim Davidson

Lily Savage

Max Bygraves

Name That Tune

Cilla Black

Dusty Springfield

Freddie Starr

Jack Jones

Sammy Davis Jnr.

Top Of The Pops (19 years)

Benny Hill (22 years)

Mike Yarwood

Des O'Connor

Michael Barrymore

Miss World x 10

Royal Command x 10

Eurovision Song Contest x 2

Seaside Special

Holiday On Ice

Jimmy Tarbuck

Lulu

Cliff Richard

Game for a Laugh

Signature Tunes

Hi De Hi
Blankety Blank
Chance In A Million

T.V. Jingles

Opal Fruits
Murray Mints
Fairy Liquid
Hoover
Pepsodent
Robinson's Jam
Camay
John Collier
Comford
Rael-Brook Toplin
Shell
Esso
Heinz beans
Bird's Eye Fish Fingers
Wall's Cornetto

Footnote: As a self-confessed amnesiac, I have compiled these listings in good faith, aware that there are probably many more, long forgotten!!

Maggie